W9-BES-664

it's your choice

The Practical Guide to Planning a Funeral

Thomas C. Nelson

Foreword by Claude Pepper

American Association of Retired Persons
Scott, Foresman and Company
Lifelong Learning Division
Glenview, Illinois

Copyright © 1983
Scott, Foresman and Company, Glenview, Illinois
American Association of Retired Persons, Washington, D.C.
All Rights Reserved
Printed in the United States of America
  23456-KPF-86858483

Library of Congress Cataloging in Publication Data

Nelson, Thomas C.
  It's Your Choice

    1. Funeral rites and ceremonies—United States—
  Handbooks, manuals, etc.   I. American Association of
  Retired Persons.   II. Title.
  GT3203.A2N44   1983   393'.0973   82-10404

  ISBN 0-673-24804-6

This publication is protected by Copyright and permission
should be obtained from the publisher prior to any prohibited
reproduction, storage in a retrieval system, or transmission in
any form or by any means, electronic, mechanical, photocopy-
ing, recording, or otherwise. For information regarding permission, write to: Scott, Foresman and Company, 1900 East Lake
Avenue, Glenview, Illinois 60025.

CONTENTS

This book is an educational and public service project of the American Association of Retired Persons which with a membership of more than 13 million is the largest association of middle-aged and older persons in the world today. Founded in 1958, AARP provides older Americans with a wide range of membership programs and services, including legislative representation at both federal and state levels. For further information about additional association activities, write to AARP, 1909 K Street, N.W., Washington, DC 20049.

FOREWORD

OLDER AMERICANS TODAY comprise the fastest growing minority group in the nation—and the only minority group of which we shall all eventually become members, providing we live long enough. It wasn't always this way. When I first came to Washington as an elected legislator in 1936, there were approximately eight million people over the age of 65 in the entire country; now, there are more than 1.5 million in my own home state of Florida alone, and a total of some 25 million in all 50 states.

Throughout my tenure in the Congress, I have been honored to deal with the concerns of our nation's elders, and have been gratified to watch public awareness of both the problems and potential of older Americans increasing steadily in appropriate proportion to their constantly growing presence in the nation's populace. More recently, this awareness has been accompanied by a growing recognition of the importance of older consumers in the American marketplace.

There are special areas of commerce which are almost exclusively the concern of middle-aged and older Americans and their families. One such area is the making of funeral arrangements and the cost—both financial and emotional—of this final and most difficult purchase.

A funeral can be one of the most expensive expenditures (after a home and a car) a consumer may make in the course of a lifetime; for many older consumers it may in fact be the *most* expensive expense they have ahead. This expense comes at a time when most of us are grief-stricken and thus psychologically vulnerable to becoming easy prey for unethical salespersons. After journalist and social critic Jessica Mitford exposed

The American Way of Death to public scrutiny in her classic book of the same title, Congress investigated the situation in 1964, but few, if any, concrete reforms emerged.

Nearly a decade later, in the early 1970s, the Federal Trade Commission began its nationwide investigation of the American funeral industry. This inquiry resulted in the passage of a set of trade regulation rules which, as a result of political intervention in the regulatory process, were considerably weaker than those originally proposed by the FTC.

All of these legislative and regulatory efforts, however, are secondary, in my view, to the best possible solution to any situation of this sort—an informed consumer. Unfortunately, planning a funeral is a subject about which few of us are inclined to seek out much information in advance, especially if we don't know how to go about doing so.

In *It's Your Choice: The Practical Guide to Planning a Funeral*, Thomas C. Nelson, who is in charge of consumer affairs at AARP and previously helped conduct the FTC's funeral investigation, has put together in one place virtually everything you need to know about funeral prices, options, and legal requirements. The book is part of a growing series of consumer action programs being developed by the American Association of Retired Persons to assist older Americans in coping with the challenges of the marketplace.

By presenting this vital information in an interesting and readable format, Nelson has created an indispensable tool for enabling concerned consumers to become informed consumers. It doesn't matter whether you want the most ornate or the simplest funeral available; what is important is that you be able to purchase what you desire at the fairest price possible. The book provides the information needed for making a free and informed choice when the time comes. Most of us will have to make funeral arrangements someday; all of us should read *It's Your Choice* now.

Congressman Claude Pepper
Chairman, House Select Committee on Aging

PREFACE

A FUNERAL CAN be an expensive and difficult purchase. Many of us are forced to make decisions about funeral arrangements for relatives or friends when we are most overcome by grief and unsure of what to do. Some people may find it troubling to preplan their own funeral, but planning ahead is the best way to assure that whoever arranges your funeral, whether it be a relative, friend, attorney, or clergy person, will handle it in the way you deem most meaningful. Securing information in advance about costs, requirements, and funeral options can reduce confusion or uncertainty later. Writing down your funeral wishes and discussing them with your probable survivors will reduce the burden on them by letting them know how you would like things conducted.

This planning book is designed to help you think about and plan your funeral needs in advance, or to assist you if you are making funeral arrangements after the death of a relative or friend. It does not attempt to sell a particular kind of funeral, expensive or inexpensive. It does not contain advice on religious issues or other personal questions, nor does it try to tell you what will be most meaningful to you. It does not in any way take the place of a will. What this planning book does is to provide the practical information you will need to act as an informed consumer.

Thinking of the person who is arranging a funeral as a consumer reflects not a lack of appreciation for the personal or religious aspects of the funeral but rather a realization that any purchase that may cost as much as $2,500 (or more) is, at least in part, a consumer purchase. This is to say that in order to make secure and appropriate decisions, you need consumer viii

information on options and price differences, just as for any other purchase. And being an informed consumer is your best assurance of getting what you want at the price you want to pay.

This book is an outgrowth of this belief and of AARP's ongoing commitment to consumer advocacy through education. Since the early 1970s, AARP has actively advocated regulation of the nation's funeral industry at both state and federal levels, and was deeply involved in the Federal Trade Commission's investigation of funeral industry practices. The lessons of such involvement have reconfirmed the Association's conviction that, if consumers are to be able to exercise their hard-won rights effectively, education must be an essential complement to regulation. That, then, is the mission of this volume.

For their assistance in the development of this book, the author is grateful to . . .

Funeral directors in New York, California, and Maryland for whom he worked part-time while in college and graduate school. These experiences gave him on-the-job experience and a growing interest in this unique consumer purchase.

Good friends and colleagues from four years of working on the Federal Trade Commission's investigation of the funeral industry who aided his efforts to further understand this transaction.

In southern California, association members, Frances Beaumont, Ella Cooper, John Fiscus, John Hinton, Golda Larks, and Ed Skaring, who served on an advisory committee once the writing of this book was underway.

Jean Nalibow of the Association's area office in Long Beach, California, who provided straightforward counsel on the manuscript's early drafts. Anne Harvey, Paul Kerschner, and other members of AARP's headquarters staff, who gave not only insightful criticism but the ongoing support necessary to make this project possible. Dr. J. Carlton Green, a retired minister and college professor from Grand Forks,

North Dakota, who offered a thorough review of the manuscript in its later stages.

And always, Kathryn Nelson, who gave the honest editing and rewriting assistance which only a spouse is best able to provide.

Acknowledgment is gratefully extended to the following for permission to reprint their materials:

Examples of funeral costs from FUNERAL INDUSTRY PRACTICES. Final Staff Report to the Federal Trade Commission and Proposed Trade Regulations Rule (16 CFR Part 453). Bureau of Consumer Protection, June 1978.

Examples of memorial society prices from "Did you ever stop to think . . . ," CONSUMER FUNERAL INFORMATION PROJECT brochure, Los Angeles Funeral Society, Inc., Panorama City, CA.

Listing of whole-body or organ donation resource groups from A MANUAL OF DEATH EDUCATION AND SIMPLE BURIAL, Ninth Edition, by Ernest Morgan. Copyright 1980 by Celo Press ($2.50 plus $1.00 postage from Celo Press, Route 5, Burnsville, NC 28714). It is also available for $3.50 including postage from CAFMS (Continental Association of Funeral and Memorial Societies), 1828 L St., Suite 1100 Washington, DC 20036.

Listing of memorial societies in the United States and Canada from the pamphlet DIRECTORY OF MEMBER SOCIETIES. Copyright 1982. Reprinted by permission. Copies available free from CAFMS (address above).

Price Comparison Forms adapted from Consumer Survey Handbook 3, THE PRICE OF DEATH, A Survey Method and Consumer Guide for Funerals, Cemeteries and Grave Markers. Seattle Regional Office of the Federal Trade Commission, December 1975.

The author is grateful to all who have helped. His hope is that this book will aid many in realizing that, when it comes time to make funeral arrangements, there are indeed choices.

About the Author

Thomas C. Nelson knows and understands the funeral industry from both inside and out. As a staff member of the Federal Trade Commission's Bureau of Consumer Protection, he worked on the agency's nationwide investigation of the funeral industry. Earlier, while a student in Union College and Columbia University, he worked part time at several funeral homes and was involved in all phases of the operations.

Nelson is currently in charge of the consumer affairs program of the American Association of Retired Persons. Previously he served as a consultant to the FTC's Office of Policy Planning for whom he prepared a report on the problems and needs of older Americans.

Chapter One

A UNIQUE SITUATION

EVEN WITH PREPLANNING, a number of factors interact to make the purchasing of funeral services and merchandise a unique experience. Without preplanning, the situation becomes even more complicated. The sheer number of details that seem to need taking care of following a death can seem overwhelming, and the decisions to be made are often unclear. Under these circumstances, the consumer often arranges for more services or purchases more expensive merchandise than is needed or desirable and frequently pays more than is necessary as well.

This chapter will provide an overview of some of the factors that contribute to this unique situation.

A Closer Look

In many cases a bereaved and less-than-clearheaded consumer is faced with purchasing services and merchandise from a funeral director who is thoroughly familiar with the situation and well prepared to meet its demands. This creates a serious imbalance in what might have been, with preplanning, a more normal purchasing situation. Seeing this situation from both sides can provide a useful background to the actual decisions to be made.

Consumer Vulnerability

The bereaved individual who is arranging for a funeral is often in a very vulnerable position. He or she will probably be plagued by a variety of feelings and pressures that will make selecting a funeral a difficult experience. Immediately after a death, emotional trauma may cause a survivor to become confused, disoriented, or numbed by shock. The best protection that a bereaved person can have during this period is the concern of a close friend. If you have to make funeral arrangements, take with you a friend or family member who is less distraught, or a family counselor such as a member of the clergy or an attorney. Be sure to take along someone whose judgment you respect and whose opinions you will listen to when emotional trauma may cloud your thinking.

Guilt is a normal emotion commonly present when funeral arrangements are made. Guilt may prompt a person to buy an expensive casket or to order "nothing but the best." It may also be something an unethical funeral director will play upon, perhaps very subtly, to sell expensive goods and services. While purchasing an expensive funeral may be one way to resolve guilt, there are other less costly and more positive ways. You should sort out your feelings before going to a funeral home. Again, taking a trusted friend is excellent protection, since bereaved persons often find themselves highly dependent upon the advice of others. It is far better to rely on the advice of a less emotionally involved friend than solely on that of a funeral director who, as a business person, is concerned with selling merchandise and services.

Another factor that may prompt a bereaved survivor to act without fully considering options is the pressure of time. Hospitals or nursing homes may require that the body be moved almost immediately after death, or you may simply want to "do something" to get this difficult task under way and over with. But the need to act quickly may mean acting foolishly, so you should delay making decisions until you are ready.

The most common element, however, contributing to an individual's difficulty in making funeral arrangements, either in advance or at the time of need, is a lack of information about funeral prices, options, and requirements. Few of us go looking for funeral information. It is rare that we will talk about funeral prices with our friends, and concrete price information has not been widely available. Consequently, ignorance may prevent us from obtaining the type of funeral we desire.

Funeral Merchandising

Often funeral directors present customers with what is essentially a funeral package for a set price. This planning book attempts to break that package apart to let you decide about each item on its own merits so that you can select exactly the type of funeral you desire at the price with which you are comfortable. Many things go into making a decision: personal preference, local custom, price, and legal requirements. Here you will find the factual information you need or instructions on how to get it, but it is up to you to take account of your own feelings and wishes.

While funeral consumers may be in a disadvantaged position, funeral directors are not. They have experience, information, and education on their side. They can greatly assist you in making important decisions and in taking care of many details. But you must not lose sight of the fact that a funeral director is a business person who must constantly pay attention to finances.

There are currently about 22,000 funeral homes in the United States. Since roughly two million persons die each year, the average number of deaths per funeral home is fewer than 100 per year (of course some have many more and some even fewer). The economics should be clear. The maintenance of an attractive, up-to-date facility, new limousines and hearses, and an adequate staff creates high overhead costs that must be recovered on a relatively small number of funerals.

The funeral director therefore has a strong economic incentive to sell expensive funerals.

But there are other reasons that funeral directors may try to sell you an expensive, "complete" funeral. Like many of us, they believe in what they are doing. They may think that their services and facilities are the best for you. Each may feel that you will be best served by following his or her recommendations. You certainly are free to do that if you choose, but the philosophy underlying this planning book is that you should know the choices. As an informed consumer, you will be free to follow a funeral director's recommendations or not, based on what *you* think is best.

There are basically three types of funeral consumers: (1) the individual who is planning his or her own funeral in advance, (2) the grief-stricken survivor arranging the funeral of a family member or close friend, and (3) the professional person, frequently an attorney, arranging a funeral on behalf of a deceased client. The information in this book can be used by all three, and the planning forms in Appendix D can serve either as an aid in preplanning or as a guide to survivors.

Reading and using this book carefully will create a balance in your relationship with a funeral director. It will enable you to use the offered expertise and advice in the best way possible, because you too will be informed.

REMEMBER: ◆ *It is perfectly normal for a bereaved consumer to experience feelings of guilt, confusion, and uncertainty about what to do.* ◆ *A clear-thinking friend or relative should accompany a bereaved consumer when funeral arrangements are made.* ◆ *A funeral director is first and foremost a business person concerned with selling services and merchandise.*

Basic Decisions

Now having some background to the situation, you are in a better position to tackle some basic decisions. If you are preplanning your own funeral, you will need to decide three very important things: (1) the kind of final disposition that will be made, (2) the kind of funeral ceremony (if any) that will take place, and (3) who will handle the arrangements. If you are responsible for making arrangements after the death of someone close to you, you may first want to call a member of the clergy or an attorney, but you will also need to decide these same three things. The outcome of these three decisions will determine all subsequent actions.

There are alternatives available, and you should thoughtfully consider each of them before beginning a course of action. Note that at each decision point, one outcome may preclude certain options at other points. If the remains, for example, are donated to a medical school, this will usually make embalming and a funeral ceremony with the body present impossible. Similarly, if you adhere to a particular religious tradition, this may dictate the outcomes of some decisions. Cremation, for example, is not allowed by some religious groups.

Disposition

Whether you decide to have a funeral ceremony or not, a decision about the kind of disposition must be made.

Burial Traditionally, most people have chosen earth burial. Many families have family plots where generations of their members have been buried. Many consumers purchase burial plots in cemeteries well in advance of need. (See pages 52–57 for a discussion of cemeteries.) If you choose earth burial, you will probably need to purchase not only a plot but also a grave liner or vault and to pay for the opening and closing of the grave and cemetery upkeep.

Cremation While more people in the United States are buried than cremated, cremation is an acceptable and increasingly popular option for many people. A survey of older people in several Florida communities found that twenty-eight percent desired cremation. (See pages 19–20 for more detailed information about cremation.)

Either burial or cremation can be performed soon after death and then followed, if desired, by a service or ceremony without the body present. This direct disposition is less expensive than a funeral service with the body present since many of the services and facilities of the funeral director are not used. (See pages 18–19 for details on direct disposition.) After cremation there may be charges for disposition of the ashes through burial or scattering, but usually cremation is somewhat less expensive than the purchase of a cemetery plot and casket. Keep in mind, though, that the expense of a funeral is determined not only by the kind of final disposition but also by the kind of service and the degree to which you use a funeral director's services, staff, facilities, and merchandise.

Donation of Remains to a Research Institution Donation of the body to a medical or dental school for research or education is another disposition alternative. The costs associated with this type of disposition are usually minimal, but arrangements must be made in advance. Alternative plans are also advisable in case the research institution cannot accept a body at the time of death. (Pages 18–21 discuss how to arrange for medical school donation.)

Funeral Ceremony

Unless a whole-body donation is made or the body is otherwise unavailable (as after an accident, for example), the choices of funeral ceremonies usually range from a traditional funeral with embalming, viewing, and a religious service with the body present to a simple disposition of the body with a memorial service or no service at all. If a traditional service is selected, it may be very lavish and expensive or very simple and inexpensive.

Many people choose something between direct disposition and a traditional funeral. For example, you might decide to forgo viewing and a church service with the body present, but wish to have a graveside service with close family present and then a memorial service for the wider circle of family and friends. Another option might be to decide against viewing or calling hours but in favor of a church funeral with the body present in a closed casket.

Embalming

One decision that will be related to the kind of funeral ceremony selected is whether or not to have embalming performed. Many studies have disclosed widespread confusion about the need for and reason for embalming. It is discussed in detail on pages 32–34, but you should know at the outset that you do have a choice about embalming. It is necessary only in certain circumstances; for example, some states require embalming when death occurs from diseases such as cholera or bubonic plague or when the burial or cremation is not accomplished within a certain length of time.

If you wish to have viewing of the body for several days before the funeral, embalming will probably be necessary. If there is to be no viewing and a closed casket at the funeral, other methods of temporary preservation, such as refrigeration, may be adequate. It may also be possible for the family or close friends to view the body one last time soon after death without embalming. The body may not have the almost lifelike appearance of being asleep that is achieved through embalming and cosmetics, but it is viewable in many cases. The point is that *you do have a choice*. Make your wishes known early (at your very first contact with the funeral director), since many funeral homes routinely embalm whether or not the consumer has requested it.

REMEMBER: ◆ *Cremation or burial can be either direct or after a traditional funeral service.* ◆ *If you choose a direct disposition (cremation or burial), it will be less expensive than disposition after a full funeral service.* ◆ *Your options cover a wide range, from a conventional funeral to donation of the remains to a medical school without any kind of service.* ◆ *Explore the options that you feel are appropriate. Make your wishes known through preplanning and by discussing your plans with those who will likely survive you.* ◆ *Embalming is required only in certain circumstances.* ◆ *If you do not desire embalming, make your wishes known at the earliest contact with the funeral director.*

Immediate Steps After Death Occurs

The first steps to be taken after a death occurs involve removal of the remains and the search for the various other services that will be necessary.

Removal

The first real decision that must be made, and in many ways the most important one, concerns whom to call when death occurs. If the remains or certain organs have been willed or donated to a medical school, organ bank, or similar facility, the organization involved should be contacted immediately upon death. Timely removal of donated organs is crucial if they are to be useful to others.

If donation is not the disposition of choice, you may need some time to make the basic decisions about arrangements. In some instances a hospital or nursing home will hold the body if you are undecided. When the facility cannot accommodate your need for more time, the body can be removed temporarily to a funeral home while you are deciding which establishment will actually handle the funeral. In such a case, you should make it clear that you are asking the funeral director only to pick up the body and hold it while you decide what kinds of arrangements you want and which facility to use. There will most likely be a charge for this service of picking up, holding, and transferring the body to the funeral home or other location you finally select. It may be a worthwhile expense, however, rather than committing yourself when you are unsure of just what final arrangements you will make. Find out, in advance, what the charge will be. You always have the right to change funeral homes even if a particular funeral director tries to discourage you from doing so.

Facilities and Services
Once the decisions on disposition and kind of ceremony have been made, you may be in the position of having to choose among several funeral homes or disposition companies to make arrangements.

Funeral Homes You can request a funeral home, or mortuary, to pick up the remains, and then meet with the funeral director to arrange the kind of funeral you desire. The choice of funeral home may be dictated by any number of considerations: past experience, location, attractiveness of facilities, personal acquaintance with the funeral director, or price. There is certainly nothing wrong with checking funeral prices and options before you commit yourself to a particular funeral home. You would probably do such checking before making any other major purchase. Since funeral home prices vary depending on the facility and on your choice of merchandise and services, you may be able to save money by doing some comparing. In many instances this can be done over the telephone. The Price Comparison Guide in Appendix C should help you in asking the right questions and checking prices.

Immediate Disposition Companies Some areas have immediate disposition companies that often advertise on the obituary pages of newspapers. They may charge a small membership fee, but generally they offer inexpensive ($200–$500), simple dispositions including pickup and delivery of the body to place of disposition (crematory or cemetery), actual disposition, and completion of the necessary paperwork. They do not offer conventional funeral-home facilities for viewing or a ceremony with the body present.

Memorial and Funeral Societies
It may be very useful to contact one of these nonprofit societies that exist in many communities to serve as intermediaries between consumers and funeral directors. They do not actually provide funeral services but refer members to cooperating funeral directors to obtain inexpensive but adequate funerals. Generally, there is a small ($10–$20) one-time membership fee. In most instances membership must be taken out prior to need, although some societies

permit membership after a death on behalf of the deceased. (See Appendix B for a list of memorial societies.)

REMEMBER: ◆ *Try to consider all your options before selecting a particular establishment to handle the funeral and disposition.* ◆ *You may want to investigate the services of direct disposition companies or memorial societies in your area.*

Special Circumstances

Sometimes special circumstances require other decisions to be made soon after death.

Death Far from Home

If death occurs away from the place where the funeral is to be held or disposition made, it may be necessary to ship the remains by air, sea, or rail. A funeral director can arrange this and will inform you of the charges. You can contact a funeral director either in the place where the death occurs or at the final destination to make the necessary arrangements. Find out whether there will be a markup or service charge in addition to the airline or railroad charge. If there is a markup, you may want to look for another funeral director who does not apply one.

If the remains must be shipped, you will likely have to pay for services provided by the funeral director who ships the body and the one who receives it. Be careful that, between the two, you are not billed twice for the same service, especially embalming. Also do not allow yourself to be sold two caskets unless you want a simple one for shipping and a more elaborate one for the service.

It is worth noting that most memorial societies will provide assistance to members of other societies when a death occurs away from home.

Death Overseas

Death in a country overseas presents a unique set of considerations that must be dealt with. Local rules and regulations will have to be followed. The first step is to contact the appropriate staff person at the nearest American embassy or consulate. This person will be in the best position to advise you about local requirements and the options available to you. You may be able to have the body embalmed and shipped home, cremated and the ashes shipped home, or buried in the country where the death occurs. Your choice will depend not only on your wishes but also on that country's regulations and facilities. For example, embalming is unheard of in some areas. The embassy or consular staff person also will be able to assist you in securing, or possibly advancing, the funds necessary to complete the arrangements.

Chapter Two

OPTIONS: DISPOSITIONS AND CEREMONIES

THIS CHAPTER discusses in more detail the various choices for disposition of the body and for funeral ceremonies.

First Considerations

Before dealing with matters relating to either disposition or the funeral ceremony, however, you should know more about memorial societies, which can make any kind of funeral planning easier, and about the possibility of funerals without the services of a funeral director.

Memorial Societies

These nonprofit membership groups are an option for making sure you get the kind of funeral you want at a reasonable price. The more than two hundred local memorial societies throughout the United States and Canada have nearly one million members. As stated previously, you can join a memorial society in your community by paying a small one-time membership fee (usually between $10 and $20). In Appendix B, in addition to a list of local societies are the addresses of the national headquarters of the organizations to which bona fide societies usually belong.

A memorial society is organized and run by volunteers. It does not provide any merchandise or funeral services directly; rather it seeks contracts with cooperating funeral directors to take care of the needs of the membership. Usually a funeral director will agree to provide simple funeral services for members at a set price. The memorial society price is often substantially below what is available to nonmembers. Upon contacting a society, you receive information about the available services and the prices offered by cooperating funeral directors (see page 30 for an example of a memorial society's plans and prices).

Traditionally, memorial society members have shown a preference for cremation, but now many societies offer members a choice of simple traditional funerals at modest, pre-negotiated prices. Upon joining a society, you will be able to indicate your preference for one of these plans. There is no requirement that you prepay anything, but there will be strong encouragement from the society for you to preplan.

You are free to cancel your membership at any time. If you move to another location, a transfer of your membership can usually be arranged at little or no additional charge. Likewise, as was noted earlier, if death occurs away from home, the local society at the place of death will usually be willing to provide assistance.

If interested, you should join a memorial society in advance so that you will have the opportunity to preplan. Many societies, however, will accept a posthumous membership on behalf of a deceased person. You may call a society immediately after the death, explain the situation, and request assistance. Even if the society cannot accept a posthumous membership, it may be able to give you some sound advice on how to go about making arrangements in your area.

You should be careful not to confuse profit-making businesses and memorial societies just because a business uses the word *society* or *memorial* in its name. Authentic societies do not sell services or merchandise directly, do not charge high membership fees, and usually belong to the Continental Association of Funeral and Memorial Societies.

Funerals Without a Funeral Director

In some areas it is possible for family members or friends to take care of all the details of the funeral and the disposition without the services of a funeral director. The St. Francis Burial and Counseling Society (see page 69) can provide information on this option. (The St. Francis Society also provides simple caskets directly to the public as well as kits and instructions for building a casket.)

Without a funeral director, it will be necessary to take care of a number of details as well as the handling of the body. For example, a death certificate will have to be completed and filed according to local regulations, a casket procured if needed, and arrangements finalized with a crematory or cemetery. Thus a great deal of careful thought and planning should be done before attempting to take care of a disposition without the assistance of a funeral director. Also, in some areas there may be regulations that require a funeral director to be involved, for example, in the transportation of the body.

REMEMBER: ◆ *Memorial societies are an option worth investigating if you are interested in a low-cost and simple funeral or disposition.* ◆ *Not all organizations with the word* memorial *or* society *in their names are true non-profit groups; investigate first.* ◆ *In most areas it is possible (though not easy) to arrange for a funeral and disposition without a funeral director.*

Disposition of the Body

It should be mentioned that there is no right or wrong kind of funeral. You should select the kind of funeral you desire at the price you want to pay. The options available range from a lavish funeral with an expensive casket to a simple memorial service without the body present. Any one is appropriate as long as you get what you want. You may wish to select and choose primarily among the components of the traditional funeral with earth burial, but you might consider some of the alternatives. For example, more and more people are expressing a preference for cremation just as fewer and fewer seem to care about having their remains laid out for viewing. Think about all your options in advance and try to have a good idea of what you want *before* you contact a funeral director.

Direct Disposition

One inexpensive alternative is direct disposition, either burial or cremation. Direct disposition means that the body is transferred directly from the place of death to the place of disposition (cemetery or crematory). A direct disposition is less expensive than a traditional funeral because, as has been noted, few funeral director's services are used. There may be no embalming, no viewing, no need for an expensive casket. After the disposition, a memorial service or services of remembrance can be held at a church or synagogue, funeral home, family home, or other meeting place.

A direct disposition followed by cremation is less expensive than one followed by burial because cemetery costs (for the plot, opening and closing, marker, and so on) are higher than crematory charges (usually between $75 and $200). Of course you can buy an expensive container (an urn) for the ashes and have them buried in a plot or placed in a special building (columbarium). A bronze urn might cost $100 or more and a niche in a columbarium can cost from $50 to more than $1,000.

Funeral directors as well as direct disposition companies (which usually charge a membership fee) can generally provide the necessary services. Remember that direct disposition companies often advertise on newspaper obituary pages. If you talk with a funeral director, be wary of being talked out of a direct disposition and into a traditional funeral. Know what you want, and make sure that you get it. Direct dispositions cost around $300. This usually includes the cost of cremation but does not include the purchase of a cemetery plot if you desire earth burial.

Earth Burial
Still the most common form of disposition in the United States and Canada, earth burial is the interment in a grave, or crypt, of uncremated remains in a casket or other suitable container. Earth burial can take place after a funeral ceremony elsewhere, after a simple graveside service, or as part of a direct disposition when there is no service at all.

Earth burial can be an expensive part of the funeral arrangements. In addition to buying a cemetery plot (though many persons already have space available in a family plot), you may have to pay for the opening and closing of the grave, a grave liner or vault, a marker, and and so on. Cemetery prices and related items are discussed in detail on pages 52–57.

Entombment
Entombment is the placement of the casket with the remains in a mausoleum, or above-ground tomb. Although some families have family tombs in cemeteries, most persons who choose entombment will need to select space in a mausoleum and deal with a cemetery for this purchase. This is discussed in more detail on page 55.

Cremation
Cremation, which is available in most areas, reduces the body to ashes. These ashes can be buried or scattered, depending on your wishes and on municipal restrictions, which may prohibit scattering near water or on public property.

Cremation after a conventional funeral is possible, but it will be far more costly than direct disposition. You can arrange for a complete funeral with embalming, viewing, and a ceremony with the body present to be followed by cremation. Compared with burial, however, cremation will usually be a less expensive form of disposition. Some funeral homes and crematories may require you to buy a casket for an immediate cremation. No state has a law that requires that a casket be used for cremation, and you should consider using another funeral home or crematory if you do not wish to purchase a casket. Containers that are perfectly suitable for direct cremation are available at little cost.

There are, however, reasons other than cost for deciding for or against cremation. Some persons feel that cremation is ecologically more desirable. Others prefer it to being buried in the ground, while many simply prefer burial. If a death is of a suspicious nature, the law may require that cremation be delayed. Most religious groups approve cremation, but some, such as Eastern Orthodoxy, Islam, Orthodox Judaism, and certain theologically conservative Protestant denominations, do not.

Whole-Body and Organ Donation

The donation of one's body to a medical school for research and teaching purposes is not only generous but also potentially the most economical kind of disposition. You should, however, thoroughly investigate this option in advance. The first step should be to contact the institution to which you wish to donate your remains. As you consider body donation, keep the following points in mind.

A medical school may not be willing or able to accept your donation when the time comes. A variety of reasons can prevent acceptance: donations usually cannot be accepted after an autopsy or after embalming has been performed, if major organs (with the exception of eyes) are removed, or if death is from certain diseases or a mutilating accident. Also, the medical school may simply not have a need for bodies at the time of death. Thus, it is clearly a mistake to view arranging the donation of one's body as the only plan that has to be made. You must consider other options in case your remains are not accepted.

You may have to pay transportation costs to have the remains delivered to the medical school. The Social Security lump-sum death benefit payment may cover this cost. (See pages 58–61 regarding death benefits.)

The decision to donate your body may affect other decisions, such as having the body present for the ceremony, since many institutions require that the body either not be embalmed or embalmed in a special manner. After the research or teaching is completed, the remains are usually cremated. Some schools will return the cremated remains to survivors if requested to do so; others will not. While most people view donation of one's body as a generous gift to help others, some feel it is a desecration of the human body. Some segments of the Jewish tradition oppose whole-body donation.

You can make your donation legally binding on your survivors through the provisions of the Uniform Anatomical Gift Act by properly completing a wallet-sized Uniform Donor Card, a facsimile of which is shown on page 20. Many states now have donor forms on the backs of drivers' licenses, which should be used in addition to the wallet card. You may order a free Uniform Donor Card from any of the organizations listed on page 21.

Many medical schools, however, will accept a donation only if it has been arranged in advance and if it is supported by the surviving family or relatives.

It is important to discuss your wishes with the institution and your family or friends. You can revoke your donation at any time by destroying the Uniform Donor Card and contacting the institution with which you have made arrangements.

UNIFORM DONOR CARD

OF_____

Print or type name of donor

In the hope that I may help others, I hereby make this anatomical gift, if medically acceptable, to take effect upon my death. The words and marks below indicate my desires.

I give: (a) _____ any needed organs or parts

           (b) _____ only the following organs or parts

_____

Specify the organ(s) or part(s)

for the purposes of transplantation, therapy, medical research or education;

           (c) _____ my body for anatomical study if needed.

Limitations or
special wishes, if any:_____

Signed by the donor and the following two witnesses in the presence of each other:

_____   _____

Signature of Donor   Date of Birth of Donor

_____   _____

Date Signed   City & State

_____   _____

Witness   Witness

This is a legal document under the Uniform Anatomical Gift Act or similar laws.

For further information consult your local memorial society or:

Continental Association of Funeral & Memorial Societies
1828 L Street, N.W., Washington, D.C. 20036

The Uniform Donor Card can also be used to authorize the donation of your organs. You can give broad authorization to remove any needed organs upon your death, or you can restrict the authorization to include only certain organs or elements, such as corneas, ear tissue, bone and cartilage, the pituitary gland, skin, heart valves, or kidneys. Donation of individual organs does not preclude a conventional funeral service. Again, you must make arrangements in advance by filling out the Uniform Donor Card and by discussing your wishes with your next of kin.

Since any donated organs should be removed as soon after death as possible, it is important that those close to you know of your wishes. You can get more information by contacting the Living Bank (a registry of donors), the American Medical Association, or groups such as the National Kidney Foundation or the Eye Bank Association of America, which coordinate the donation of specific organs. The addresses of all these groups are in the first section of Chapter 7.

A free Uniform Donor Card can be ordered from any one of these organizations.

Continental Association of
Funeral & Memorial Societies
1828 L Street NW
Washington, DC 20036

Eye Bank Association of America
3195 Maplewood Avenue
Winston-Salem, NC 27103

Living Bank
P.O. Box 6725
Houston, TX 77005

Medic Alert
Turlock, CA 95380

National Pituitary Agency
Suite 501-9
210 West Fayette Street
Baltimore, MD 21201

National Society for Medical
Research
1000 Vermont Avenue
Washington, DC 20005

REMEMBER: ◆ *Direct disposition and whole-body donation are two low-cost options.* ◆ *Direct disposition can be
secured from a company specializing in this kind of service
or from a cooperating funeral director.* ◆ *Be sure to investigate all possible costs associated with cremation or earth
burial.* ◆ *Arrangements for whole-body donations should
be made in advance, and you should consider alternative
forms of disposition in case your donation cannot be accepted.*

Funeral Ceremonies

While this book will focus primarily on the practical aspects of buying a funeral, it is necessary to say a little about
funeral ceremonies, because basic decisions about the kind of
ceremony desired will influence many other choices. Funeral
ceremonies provide an opportunity to commemorate the life
of the deceased and to express religious or personal beliefs
about life and death. They also allow the family and friends to
come together to remember the deceased, to express their
concern and support for each other, and to recognize the loss
that has occurred. The kind of ceremony is usually determined by personal preferences, religious beliefs, and the recommendations of clergy, family, and friends. If you are
preplanning your own funeral, it will be very helpful to your
survivors to give them some ideas about the kind of ceremony
you think most meaningful.

Some people prefer no service at all. Others want to de-
velop a unique ceremony according to their own interests and
beliefs. For still others, religious traditions will very closely
dictate the type of ceremony. If a religious ceremony is important to you, it is best to contact the clergy as soon as
possible for guidance and information about the practices of

your religion. For those who would like the participation of clergy but do not have a religious affiliation in the community, a funeral director or family friend may be able to suggest a clergy person who would be willing to perform the service.

Traditional Religious Funerals

Since there is considerable variation in funeral ceremonies within a particular religious tradition, it is almost impossible to describe in detail, for example, a "typical" Jewish funeral or a "typical" Protestant funeral. The following paragraphs, however, briefly outline the components most common in funerals of major religious groups.

Jewish Funerals The different branches of the Jewish faith—Orthodox, Conservative, and Reform—all have somewhat different funeral traditions. For Orthodox Jews there is a ritual cleansing of the body after death and prompt burial, without embalming, in a plain, all-wood casket. The ceremony includes prayers and a eulogy and usually takes place at a funeral home or synagogue with a rabbi or cantor conducting the service. The mourners accompany the casket to the cemetery for a committal service. Immediately after burial, there is a prescribed period of deep mourning called "sitting Shiva" during which members of the deceased's immediate family withdraw from the community. For up to seven days, friends and relations visit the family regularly. Any time following Shiva, the grave marker for the deceased may be unveiled, although it is customarily unveiled eleven months to one year after death.

Conservative Jews follow many of the same burial and mourning practices as Orthodox Jews, while those of the Reform tradition modify some elements. For example, some Reform Jews permit embalming and the use of nonwood caskets, and they view cremation as an acceptable option.

Regarding proposed donations of body parts to medical institutions, the family rabbi should be consulted, since reverance for the physical remains of the deceased is considered of paramount concern in Jewish law.

Catholic Funerals The local parish priest should be contacted before funeral arrangements are made. This allows for the necessary preparation for the liturgy of Christian burial, or Funeral Mass, which is the beginning point of the Catholic ceremony and is delivered in a church. During visiting hours at a funeral home prior to the funeral, a priest may conduct either a wake service or a rosary service. The liturgy of Christian burial at the church includes organ music, prayers, scripture readings, a homily, and the Eucharist. Following the Mass, worshipers proceed to the cemetery for a Christian burial service, either at graveside or interment chapel (if available). If a Mass is not celebrated, a priest may lead a service of prayers and readings at the funeral home. Although for many years cremation was not an option for Catholics, it is now acceptable, and a local parish priest will know the procedures for obtaining permission.

Protestant Funerals Given the wide variety of Protestant denominations, it is not surprising that there is tremendous diversity in Protestant funeral ceremonies. They may be held at a church or funeral home. The body may or may not be present. The service may consist of religious readings, prayers, a eulogy, and music. The committal service at the cemetery or crematory may be attended by all the worshipers or only those particularly close to the family.

Non-Judeo-Christian Funerals There are specified religious observances, rituals, and modes of disposition for non-Judeo-Christian religions such as Islam, Buddhism, and Hinduism. For example, in the Islamic faith after a service in a mosque the body is interred on its right side with the head toward Mecca. The Islamic tradition opposes cremation. However, cremation is the norm for those of the Buddhist or Hindu faith.

The preceding summaries of the types of religious funeral ceremonies are intentionally brief because the best source of information is your local minister, priest, or rabbi. You should contact him or her when you are preplanning your own funeral or after the death of a relative or friend whose funeral you must plan.

Memorial Services
The distinctive feature of a memorial service is that the body is not present. Usually a memorial service is held after a direct cremation or burial. The service can be in a church, a synagogue, a private home, a funeral home, or other meeting place. Since the body is not present, the service can be scheduled at any time that is convenient to the survivors. The actual service can be similar to a traditional funeral service or uniquely designed for the particular situation. It might, for example, consist of family and friends gathering at a family member's home for prayers and shared reminiscences about the life of the deceased. This kind of service is common among many religious groups, including Protestant congregations.

Other Kinds of Services
It is often possible to modify the traditional religious service. There are also options available to those who do not desire a religious service. Some of these modifications and nonreligious options are discussed next.

Humanist Funeral Service For those who share a humanist, nonreligious view of life and death, a service consisting of music and readings that stress kinship with nature, the ideals of human living, and the naturalness of death might be appropriate. Several of the books listed in the Further Reading section of Chapter 7 can provide guidance and suggestions about how to arrange a humanist funeral and how to select readings. This service can be conducted with or without the body present.

Fraternal Ceremonies Fraternal ceremonies conducted by groups such as the Masons or Knights of Columbus are usually held in addition to, not instead of, other funeral services. They provide the opportunity for members to pay respects to one of their group who has died.

Military Ceremonies Military ceremonies are not usually a part of the national cemetery or Veterans Administration programs. They are provided by a local military installation or by a veterans organization such as the Veterans of Foreign Wars.

REMEMBER: ◆ *Preplanning a funeral ceremony will assure the kind of service you feel is appropriate and will serve as a useful guide to your survivors.* ◆ *Consider what would be most meaningful in terms of readings, music, and participants.* ◆ *Consider in particular where to hold the service, who will officiate, what music and readings will be used, and whether or not the body will be present.* ◆ *Your local minister, priest, or rabbi is the best source of information about the funeral practices of your religious tradition.*

Whatever kind of ceremony you select (or even if you decide not to have a funeral ceremony at all), keep in mind that the most important consideration is what would be most meaningful. Feelings of guilt or pressure from even the most well-meaning friends and relatives should not determine the kind of ceremony.

Chapter Three

FUNERAL COSTS AND

BASIC SERVICES

THE BASIC DECISIONS discussed in Chapter 1 will dictate which particular services and items of merchandise you will need to purchase. For example, if you opt for direct cremation, you will make only minimal use of the funeral director's offerings. This chapter and the two that follow it contain a discussion of funeral pricing and descriptions of the major items of service and merchandise from which you can select when planning a funeral.

You have the opportunity and responsibility to choose the funeral ceremony and disposition that best meet your needs—emotionally, aesthetically, and financially. The many purchasing decisions that you will have to make are discussed in the following pages. Making these decisions in advance is your best assurance of getting what *you* want. Try not to shy away from them. Use the information contained in these pages to make knowledgeable choices to ensure that you obtain the funeral arrangements you want for yourself or for someone close to you.

Remember that for a funeral, just as for any other consumer purchase, you have to exercise your rights to secure what you want. You should not hesitate to ask questions or to request that a funeral director give you written information.

If at any point when arranging a funeral, or afterwards, you feel you have been mistreated, complain. Let the funeral director and the appropriate state authorities (listed in Chapter 7) know if you believe you have been treated unfairly.

Funeral Prices

There are basically two pricing methods used by funeral directors: package pricing and itemization. In some states, regulation establishes the kind of pricing with which funeral directors must comply.

Package Pricing

Package pricing, or unit pricing, is the quotation of a "total" price for a standard funeral. Usually this covers the "traditional" funeral, including embalming, casket, viewing, limousines, and the funeral service. The main difference between a $1,000 funeral and a $2,000 one is the kind of casket chosen. The services and facilities are the same. The package price, however, does not cover everything. You will still have to pay for such extras as cemetery expenses, grave liner, and flowers.

If you are quoted a package price, be sure to determine what is and is not included. The problem with package pricing is that it has not usually given consumers the cost of individual items; for example, embalming, viewing, and use of limousines. Some funeral directors have refused to reduce a package price even when a particular service was not used. Because of these problems, government authorities have enacted regulations requiring that at least a minimal amount of price information be available to consumers. Even so, you should still be alert to make sure that you are not charged for items or services you do not need, desire, or use.

Itemization

The pricing method called itemization gives you a separate price for each part of the funeral. This approach may seem a little more complicated, but it allows you to plan the kind of funeral you desire, knowing the cost of each item. The degree to which funeral prices are broken down varies a great deal. Some funeral homes quote casket prices separately from a package price for all services and facilities (this is called bi-unit pricing), while others give detailed prices for every part of the funeral. An October 1980 survey by the National Retired Teachers Association and the American Association of Retired Persons found that the majority of consumers prefer detailed price information, so you need not feel embarrassed about asking for it.

While the extent of price information is important, *when* you get it is even more important. It is always best to get *detailed* price information from the funeral director early in your discussion and before making any decisions. Asking about prices and being concerned about them is in no way improper or in poor taste. A funeral is an expensive purchase, and you need to know what it is going to cost. Any ethical funeral director should willingly supply you with price information in advance. If possible, request a written itemized price list of the funeral home's offerings to help you in making decisions. You should not have to guess about casket or burial vault prices. They should be prominently displayed. One very simple way to compare prices is to telephone different funeral homes. The Price Comparison Forms in Appendix C can be used for telephone as well as in-person comparisons.

Examples of Funeral Costs
While funeral costs vary a great deal, it may be useful to review several different examples of representative funeral costs. Price information, because of inflation and rising costs, becomes dated very quickly. Prices also vary greatly from one community to another. Remember, prices your funeral director or memorial society quotes can be expected to rise over the years as inflation takes its toll.

A 1978 report on funeral industry practices published by the Federal Trade Commission included a discussion of funeral prices. The typical "traditional" funeral was estimated as follows:

Funeral home charges (including casket, staff, and use of facilities)	$1,393
Interment receptacle (burial vault)	195
Obituary notice	19
Clergy honorarium	35
Death certificates	14
Cemetery expenses	555
Flowers	150
Total	$2,361

Representative of the plans that memorial societies offer through cooperating funeral directors are the following two plans offered by one California society.

Plan I: Immediate Cremation
Transportation of body to crematory, cremation, completion of necessary forms (no embalming) $247.50
Plan II: Funeral Service
Embalming, simple casket, permit to bury, transportation, viewing, and chapel or graveside service (no cemetery expenses) $583.50

The cost for services provided by an immediate-disposition company can be estimated as:

Necessary storage of the remains, transportation to the crematory, cremation, and filing of forms $250.00

These prices are meant only to give you some sense of relative funeral costs. You may find prices in your community to be very different. Also, some funeral homes can offer direct dispositions at prices competitive with immediate-disposition companies or the prices obtained by memorial societies.

REMEMBER: ◆ *Do not be embarrassed about requesting price information; you need it to make a wise decision.* ◆ *Ask for written price information early in your discussions with the funeral director. If you are quoted a package price, determine exactly what is included and what additional charges you are likely to incur.* ◆ *Try to obtain prices for the different parts of the funeral. Make sure you pay only for those items you actually use.* ◆ *If you desire, compare prices at different funeral homes before you settle on a particular establishment. The easiest way to do this is by telephone.*

Overview of the Funeral Director's Services

When you use the services of a traditional funeral director, you will have to pay for his or her time and that of the staff. The funeral director can take care of many details for you and provide some services, such as embalming, that require technical expertise. The funeral director can obtain burial permits and death certificates, contact clergy and pallbearers, place the death notice, and help you with insurance and benefits forms. During calling hours, the director or staff may be in attendance, and during the funeral ceremony they will supervise proceedings. These services may be a great help at a difficult time.

You will pay for the funeral director's services either directly or indirectly as part of the total funeral cost. According to the funeral industry, more than 30 percent of funeral costs are related to personnel expenses. If you wish to take care of some details yourself—and many people do—talk with the funeral director about having your bill reduced accordingly. For example, if you obtain the death certificates yourself or if the funeral director does not supervise calling hours (as when they are held at the family home), then you should not be charged for such services.

Arranging for direct disposition of the body straight from the place of death to the crematory or cemetery is less expensive than a traditional funeral, largely because many of the funeral director's services are not used.

REMEMBER: ◆ *The funeral director is there to assist you, but you will be charged for this assistance.* ◆ *If you wish, you should be able to use some of the funeral director's services and not others; and you should pay only for the services you use.*

Embalming and Preparation of the Body

Whether to embalm or not is an important consideration, and you should be fully aware of the reasons for your decision.

Legal Requirements

Although some funeral directors may imply otherwise, embalming is required by health regulations only in certain circumstances, primarily if death is from certain contagious diseases, if disposition of the remains is not accomplished within a specific period of time (this varies from state to state between 24 and 72 hours), or if the body is to be shipped between states. If you are thinking about declining embalming services, you may want to contact the state board of funeral directing in your state to find out exactly what the legal requirements are.

Religious Considerations
Some religions, notably Orthodox Judaism and the Islamic faith, are opposed to embalming on religious grounds.

Purpose
Embalming as currently practiced in North America does *not* provide long-term preservation of remains. Short-term preservation is desirable, however, if a funeral is going to be held with an open casket and viewing. Preservation can also be accomplished through refrigeration of the body. Some funeral directors have the necessary refrigeration equipment, and you may be charged for its use.

Personal Aesthetics
While some individuals are opposed to embalming for religious reasons, others oppose it because they feel it is a sacrilege to the body. Personal aesthetics prompt some others, however, to decide in favor of embalming because for them the presence of a lifelike body is an important part of the funeral ritual. Some people also believe that viewing the embalmed body helps survivors in dealing with grief and the sense of loss.

You do have a choice about embalming, but you must exercise it upon first contact with the funeral director. Many funeral directors routinely embalm whether this service is requested or not. It is embalming that makes a corpse viewable and necessitates the purchase of a casket in which to display the body. This in turn involves the use of the funeral director's services and facilities. So if embalming is not desired, tell the funeral director at your first contact, for example, when you request removal of the remains. If, for any reason, embalming is performed after you request that it not be, you should not be charged.

Those funeral homes that put an itemized price on embalming usually charge between $75 and $175. This fee may or may not include charges for "preparation of the body," which usually covers washing, cosmetizing, and hairdressing. If there is to be no viewing, none of these services may be necessary. On the other hand, if you decide not to have a public viewing but simply wish to have the immediate family view the body, you may want to have the body prepared but not embalmed. Be sure to ask whether there is a charge for preparation of the body in addition to embalming costs.

Dressing the remains is also part of the preparation. Burial garments are stocked and offered by most funeral directors. These are entirely optional items, however, and clothing from home can just as appropriately be used and may be more meaningful. Burial clothes can cost between $25 and $55.

REMEMBER: ◆ *You do have a choice about embalming. Decide what you want based on your preferences, the kind of funeral you select, and the legal requirements.* ◆ *It is important that you make your wishes known when you first have contact with the funeral director.* ◆ *If you do not desire embalming but wish to have a private viewing of the body, it may be possible to have only minimal preparation performed.*

Use of the Funeral Home

The extent to which you use a funeral director's facilities—and consequently, the costs that you incur—will be determined by the kind of funeral you select. There are two events for which a funeral home is often used: viewing of the body and the funeral ceremony.

Viewing

Many people hold what is known as calling hours, viewing, visitation, or a wake preceding a funeral. During this period the body, in an open or closed casket, is present, and friends and relatives stop by to pay their respects. Often this is the time when religious or fraternal services, such as a Catholic rosary service or a Masonic observance, are held. Viewing varies in length from several hours immediately preceding the funeral to a period of up to a week before the funeral. A period of two or three days for viewing is quite common.

There are alternatives to having the viewing and visitation in a funeral home. It may be possible to have the viewing in a church or private home. The funeral director, however, may charge for transporting the casket to a home or church. Or you might receive friends and family at home, church, or other meeting place without having the casket present. If you decide not to use the funeral home, speak to the funeral director about not being charged for use of the facilities.

Ceremony

A funeral home is also used by many people for the ceremony preceding burial or cremation. Alternatives might be a church or synagogue, a private home, or a fraternal meeting place. Again, when a place other than the funeral home is used, charges may be incurred for transportation of the casket, use of the facility, and the time of any funeral home employees who may be in attendance. If the funeral home itself is used for the ceremony, you will be charged for its use. Ask the funeral director about these various costs, since they may be one factor in your decision about where to hold the funeral. But in addition to price, you should consider where the service will be most meaningful to you, the availability of other facilities, and convenience.

Your decision about whether or not to have the body present will also play a part in deciding where to hold the funeral ceremony. If the body is to be present, a funeral home or a church may be most convenient. If it is not, you will have greater flexibility about where to hold the service.

REMEMBER: ◆ *You will need to decide whether providing the opportunity for friends and family to call is important to you.* ◆ *If you opt for visitation, you will have to decide whether the body should be present.* ◆ *You should decide on where to hold the visitation and ceremony. A funeral home may be the most convenient, but other places, such as a church or private home, may be more meaningful or less expensive.* ◆ *Find out in advance the charges for using different facilities.*

Chapter Four

ADDITIONAL SERVICES

IN ADDITION to the services discussed in the previous chapter, the funeral director is prepared to offer a variety of services related to the funeral ceremony itself, to the transportation of the remains afterwards, and to various paperwork tasks. These services are covered here.

Services Related to the Funeral Ceremony

Music and flowers have long been staples of traditional funerals. The funeral director can help arrange these as well as provide other services during the funeral ceremony.

Music

Many people believe that music can be both meaningful and comforting at a funeral ceremony. Such musicians as an organist, a singer, or both are often used, but taped music is not uncommon. You should find out what the charge is for these services and decide what best meets your needs.

You might also consider having a talented friend or relative provide the music. This could be more meaningful and would not involve fees for a professional musician.

Flowers and Charitable Contributions

Many people feel that flowers add a beautiful touch to a funeral ceremony and are a meaningful way of showing respect and sympathy. Others feel that flowers are an expensive and short-lived gesture and that there are more appropriate ways to express sorrow, such as donations to charity. Your preference for flowers or contributions to charity can be indicated in the planning forms in Appendix D.

Flowers for a funeral can range from several roses on the casket to elaborate sprays and baskets. In some communities it is traditional for the immediate family to provide a flower piece for the casket, and for friends and other family members to purchase other arrangements. People can spend less than fifty dollars to many hundreds of dollars on funeral flowers.

If you decide to order flowers, you can usually deal directly with a florist. The funeral director can, however, take care of ordering for you. You can select the kind of flowers, color, and style of arrangement you wish. As always, remember to get what you want at the price you want. If you have the funeral director handle the flowers, find out whether a service charge or markup is added to the florist's charges. If it is, it may make sense to deal directly with a florist.

An increasingly popular alternative to sending flowers is to give a donation to charity in memory of the deceased. The representatives of most charities will be happy to discuss the options they have available for memorial gifts and will send an acknowledgment of the gift to the deceased's family. Sometimes special funds, such as a scholarship, are set up to receive gifts in memory of a particular individual. Local charities, your church or synagogue, and educational or medical institutions can provide more information on memorial giving. It is usually possible to include in the death notice an indication that the family prefers contributions to be made to a particular charity. A combination of flowers and memorial gifts is not uncommon.

You may wish to consider an additional type of memorialization, such as planting a tree, donating a new bench in a favorite park, or buying hymnals for a church or a new piece of equipment for the local school or senior-citizens group. These kinds of memorials do provide ongoing benefits to others and a meaningful way to remember the deceased. If you are preplanning your funeral, it will greatly assist your survivors if you furnish them with some guidance as to how you would like to be remembered.

Guestbooks, Acknowledgment Cards, Prayer Cards, and Programs

Materials such as guestbooks (to record who comes to the funeral home or ceremony) and acknowledgment cards (to express your appreciation for gifts and other gestures of sympathy) are provided as a service at some funeral homes. Prayer cards and programs may also be printed. You may find some of these items useful, but since you may be charged for them, you should find out what they cost. If you decide that you need or want them, you may want to find out whether you can get them elsewhere for less money.

Honoraria and Gratuities

You may want to (you sometimes are required to) provide an honorarium or gratuity to certain persons such as the clergy and musicians who provide services during the funeral ceremony. The individual minister, priest, or rabbi, the church or synagogue office, or the funeral director can help you decide what is appropriate. You can either give the honorarium directly to the individual or to the church or synagogue or have the funeral director handle it.

Tape Recordings

Some funeral directors now offer to record the funeral service and to sell copies of the recording to survivors. Since survivors are sometimes too distraught to fully appreciate the actual service, such a recording may be of interest. If you do not wish to purchase a tape from the funeral director, you should have the option of asking a friend or relative to take responsibility for recording the ceremony.

Nurse
At some funerals, a nurse is in attendance to provide assist-ance if it is needed. He or she may be a registered nurse, licensed practical nurse, or a nursing assistant. If you desire to have such a person available, the funeral director can make necessary arrangements.

Transportation of Remains to Cemetery

When a casket with the remains must be transported after a ceremony from a funeral home or other location to a ceme-tery for burial or entombment, another group of services is often needed. Pallbearers and a hearse are almost always used. Flower cars, limousines, and police escorts may or may not be used. If the remains must be transported a great distance, shipping by train or airplane may be necessary.

Pallbearers
One way that friends and family can participate in the funeral ceremony if the casket is present is to serve as pallbearers. You can indicate the individuals that you would like to per-form this honor in the Personal Planning Forms in Appendix D. You normally need to select six pallbearers. The funeral director will explain to the pallbearers what they need to do and when. In addition to those who actually carry the casket, it is possible to have honorary pallbearers who accompany it.

If you do not use friends or acquaintances as pallbearers, it may be necessary to hire "professional" ones. The funeral director can arrange this service and tell you what the charge will be. The help of the funeral-home staff may be available without a direct charge. In a few areas, such as New York City, unions require the use of paid pallbearers.

Hearse

The hearse, which carries the casket, is a familiar part of the funeral procession. If the funeral director's charges are itemized, you can find out exactly what the hearse costs you. If they aren't, the hearse will be included in the package price. Separate charges may be made for picking up the remains at the place of death and transporting them to the funeral home. Sometimes additional charges are made if the hearse has to travel a long distance. Some funeral directors will allow use of a less elaborate vehicle, often called a "first call" car, if you are interested in less expensive transportation.

Flower Car

At many funerals a flower car is used to transport the funeral flowers from the place of the funeral ceremony to the cemetery or crematory. You should discuss with the funeral director whether such a vehicle will be used. Find out the charge and use this service only if it is something you want and feel is necessary. Flower car charges are in the $25–$125 range.

Limousines

Some people like to use the funeral director's limousines at the time of the funeral. A limousine can pick you up at home before the funeral, provide transportation from the funeral home to the cemetery, crematory, or location of the ceremony, and return you to your home after the service. Sometimes only the immediate family rides in one or two limousines. At other times more limousines are used to provide transportation for a larger group of family members and friends.

If a funeral director uses package pricing, one or two limousines may be included. Use of more limousines will mean additional charges. Limousine charges vary in different areas and by the distance traveled. The cost per limousine

averages between $35 and $150. More and more people feel
that they do not need limousines. They prefer to drive their
own cars or have a friend drive them.

Motorcycle Escort
In some areas a motorcycle escort may be necessary when
there is to be a procession from the funeral home to the
church, cemetery, or crematory. The funeral director will tell
you whether you need this service and what the charge will
be. Rarely is such service provided by a city or town. The
off-duty police officers or private company often employed for
this service must be paid.

Shipping the Remains
Just as when death occurs away from the place where the
funeral is to be held, if the final resting place is a great
distance from the location of the funeral, it may be necessary
to ship the remains by air, sea, or rail. The funeral director
can arrange this. You will probably be charged for services
provided by the funeral director who accepts the remains at
the destination as well as those provided by the one who ships
them.

The least expensive way to ship remains is after cremation.
The ashes can be transported personally or shipped by parcel
post, air, or rail to a final location for scattering, placement
in a columbarium, or burial in a cemetery. Shipping the
remains in a casket is considerably more expensive. The body
will usually have to be embalmed and shipped in a suitable
container. Charges will be determined by weight or by the
cost of one or more required full-fare tickets.

Paperwork Services

Placing the death notice in appropriate newspapers, obtaining death certificates, and filing for death benefits are

services that the funeral director is also prepared to provide. You can, however, arrange for most if not all of these items yourself.

Death Notices and Obituaries

Most newspapers charge for carrying death notices. In some areas a newspaper will run a small death announcement free but will charge for longer obituary notices. (The often lengthy obituaries of notable persons that appear in major newspapers are considered news stories and, as such, are run at the paper's discretion and at no charge.)

The funeral director can place the death notice and can also assist you in writing an obituary if you wish to submit one to the newspaper. If the newspaper charges, the cost will be determined by the length of the story, the number of times it appears in the newspaper, and the newspaper's circulation. It may be possible to have a death notice appear both in local and in out-of-town papers. For example, you may want to have the notice appear in the town where the deceased grew up or lived and worked the longest as well as where he or she may have moved after retirement. Many people like to prepare the information that will be used in their own obituaries, such as date and place of birth, employment history, civic and religious activities, preference for memorial gifts to charity, and the names of survivors. Much of this information can be included on the planning forms in Appendix D.

If the funeral director places the death notice for you, find out whether you will be charged exactly what the newspaper charges, or whether a surcharge or markup is added. If there is an added charge, you may want to try placing the death notice for the deceased yourself, though in some areas newspapers will accept notices only from funeral directors. Persistence may or may not lead to the paper's agreeing to take the notice directly from the consumer.

Some people are electing not to have death notices published at all or are limiting the amount of information given because of the risk of burglary when the home is empty during funeral activities. It is a good idea to arrange for a friend or neighbor to stay in the home during the funeral. Or it might be possible to have the notices published after the service.

Death Certificates

Death certificates are provided by the local government office that registers deaths. Survivors will need official death certificates (simple photocopies are usually not adequate) when applying for various death benefits such as veterans or union benefits. Death certificates are also needed when applying for pension and life insurance benefits. Your attorney or funeral director can help you determine how many certificates you may need. The cost varies from area to area, but it is usually in the range of $1–$3 per certificate. Usually it is less expensive to request all you need at one time. A funeral director can obtain the certificates for you, or you can obtain them directly yourself. If a funeral director is going to obtain the certificates for you, ascertain whether or not there is a surcharge or markup on the fee charged by the issuing office. If there is, you may want to get the certificates yourself.

Death Benefits Applications

A funeral director is usually willing to assist survivors in filing for various death benefits. For example, he or she can handle the completion of the necessary paperwork for Social Security or veterans' benefits. Many persons, however, prefer to attend to these matters themselves.

REMEMBER: ◆ *For all items such as those discussed in this chapter, obtain written price information or estimates before you make your selections.* ◆ *Carefully consider your motivation for purchasing a particular item; do not be shamed or forced into purchasing something that you do not really want.* ◆ *You should not pay for services that you do not actually use.* ◆ *Determine whether or not the funeral director applies a markup or surcharge to items provided by third parties or receives discounts that are not passed on to the consumer.* ◆ *You may be able to save money by arranging for some of these additional items yourself.*

Chapter Five

CASKETS, CEMETERY PLOTS, AND OTHER PURCHASES

DEPENDING UPON what kind of final disposition is chosen, one or more items of merchandise will usually need to be purchased, in addition to the services that have been discussed. The information presented in this chapter will help you make informed selections.

Caskets

In most cases caskets are the most expensive items of funeral merchandise. They are available in a wide variety of styles and prices, ranging from a simple cardboard container that may cost as little as $25 to a solid bronze casket for many thousands of dollars. Some kind of casket usually will be necessary if earth burial or entombment is the disposition of choice. A casket may be desired by some even if cremation is to follow the funeral.

Factors in Selection
Since the sale of caskets is usually the most financially profitable part of the funeral package, some funeral directors may encourage people to buy expensive ones. So that you can select the casket that best meets your requirements, it is important for you to understand the factors that go into this decision.

Practicality Some kind of rigid container is needed for handling and transporting the body. For this purpose a simple cardboard container will usually suffice. This kind of simple container may be used when remains are shipped from one place to another. A more elaborate casket may then be purchased at the place where the funeral is held. Canvas or plastic pouches are also available for use in some circumstances.

Legal Requirements Usually there are no legal requirements affecting the kind of container that must be used. People are most often free to choose anything from the canvas pouch to the bronze sealer casket, though the law may specify a sealed casket when death results from a highly contagious disease such as cholera or yellow fever. Cemeteries or crematories, however, may have minimal standards for containers they will accept, and funeral homes may require the purchase of certain kinds of containers if there is to be viewing.

If you are told that the law requires a certain kind of container, you may want to check the law yourself by contacting the state board of funeral directing in your state. If the facility you are using (funeral home, cemetery, or crematory) requires a kind of container that you do not wish to purchase, check the requirements of other establishments.

Protection Many people buy caskets out of a desire to protect or preserve the corpse. The funeral industry realizes this and promotes some caskets (known as "sealer" caskets) as protective ones. These caskets are usually more expensive than others and often are sold with warranties or guarantees that provide for a replacement should the warranted casket "fail." Unfortunately, survivors have no idea whether or not the casket performs as claimed unless it is disinterred.

While it is true that a solid metal casket may prevent water seepage better than a cardboard container, no casket can preserve forever. In the minds of consumers, protection is often

confused with preservation. Although it is possible to purchase a casket that will protect the remains to some degree, it
is not possible to purchase one that will preserve them.

Merchandising Techniques

Since the kind of casket you select directly bears on the
expense of the funeral, you may find various sales strategies
employed to encourage you to purchase an expensive casket.
These techniques are the same ones that are used to sell other
merchandise, such as televisions and cars. Inexpensive caskets
may not be prominently displayed, or they may not be in the
display room at all. If you are interested in something less
expensive than what you see at first, ask. Inexpensive caskets
are sometimes displayed in unattractive colors. If you like a
particular casket but not the color, ask if it can be obtained in
another color. Often it can. Sometimes prices are not displayed on caskets. Do not be embarrassed about asking the
price. You need to know it to make an informed decision.

Some unethical funeral directors try to shame people into
buying expensive caskets. They may imply that worrying
about price shows a lack of respect or affection. This is only a
sales technique; you have a right and need to know about
price. Further, an interest in an inexpensive funeral says nothing about your respect or love for the deceased, nor does the
purchase of an expensive one. Some funeral directors may also
tell you that a casket should be thought of as the last gift to
the deceased. Some people may think of a casket this way,
but many can think of other ways to pay respect to the dead.
Conserving family resources also may be a way to show love
and respect.

Although most funeral directors maintain a showroom
where they display caskets, some sell caskets by showing
photographs or by taking you to a manufacturer's display
room. Before showing you the caskets, the funeral director
should explain the different kinds available.

Kinds and Prices

Following is a brief explanation of the various kinds of caskets and other containers, along with approximate retail prices for each. It is very difficult to give firm retail prices, since each funeral director applies a different markup. These prices are only examples.

Softwood Caskets Inexpensive wooden caskets are usually made of pine, plywood, or a wood composition board. They may be stained and polished, as in the case of an all-pine casket, or covered with cloth if the casket is made of plywood. Cloth-covered softwood caskets come in a wide range of colors from gray to rose. Softwood caskets are often available from $150 up.

Hardwood Caskets These caskets are made of woods such as mahogany or cherry and are usually considerably more expensive than those of softwoods. Many hardwood caskets cost a thousand dollars or more.

Sealer Metal Caskets The most expensive of the metal caskets are the "sealers," made from a heavy metal and having a sealing mechanism, usually a rubber gasket around the outside edge. Sealer caskets are promoted as protective ones, and warranties or guarantees of their protective capabilities may be available. The usefulness of such warranties, however, can be seriously questioned, as previously indicated. Sealer caskets also may be held out as offering preservation of the remains, but *they do not*. Sealer casket prices are determined in part by the thickness of the metal. Those with a thin-gauge metal are available for less than $1,000, while copper or bronze caskets may cost well over $2,000.

Nonsealer Metal Caskets These caskets are usually of lighter metal, do not have a sealing mechanism, and are less expensive than sealer caskets. They are available in a variety of colors and styles, and some are available for less than $1,000.

Alternative Containers The least expensive kind of container is the cardboard container or pouch. The pouch can be used for direct dispositions. The cardboard container is suitable for direct dispositions but may also be used if viewing or a funeral ceremony is held. Some people select the cardboard container and have it covered with a special funeral cloth (pall) during the funeral service. Fiberglass containers are also available in some areas at a higher cost than that of a pouch or cardboard container. Some funeral directors offer a casket and burial vault combination made of fiberglass.

Some funeral homes feature what is called a viewing dais, a permanent platform on which the body can be laid out for viewing. After viewing, an inexpensive container, perhaps of cardboard or composition board, is used for the actual disposition. The consumer pays for the container and rental of the dais. Likewise, a rental casket for viewing is available at some establishments, with another container used for the disposition.

REMEMBER: ◆ *A casket is an item of merchandise. It may be in a funeral director's best interest to sell you an expensive one.* ◆ *Decide on the kind of casket you want and how much you want to spend before you go to the funeral home.* ◆ *Think about why you are buying a casket. Be alert to sales pitches that appeal to your emotions, feelings of guilt, pride, or concern with the protection or "preservation" of the remains.* ◆ *If you don't see a casket you want at the price you want to spend, ask for one.* ◆ *If you are arranging for a direct disposition, think seriously about purchasing an inexpensive alternative container (of canvas or cardboard) that will adequately meet your needs.*

Urns

Cremated remains are returned to the survivors as ashes, usually in a simple cardboard box or a paper bag. If the ashes are not scattered, an urn is often purchased to hold them. The urn may then be buried in a cemetery plot, placed in a niche in a columbarium, or kept in the home.

Urns may be made of various materials, including metal, marble, and wood, and come in various sizes to hold the cremated remains of one to several people. The simplest style of urn available costs about $50, while the most expensive ones cost upwards of several thousand dollars.

Grave Liners and Burial Vaults

To lessen the chances of a grave's sinking over the years as the casket deteriorates, a grave liner or a burial vault is usually put into the open grave to receive the casket as it is lowered. A grave liner is a boxlike structure, most often made of concrete, with a loose-fitting slab cover to support the earth that will be filled in over it. A burial vault is a more substantial structure, often steel reinforced and metal lined or coated, with a tight-fitting molded lid that provides a seal when it is put into place. In many areas, cemeteries as well as funeral homes sell these items.

There are only a few local jurisdictions where legal requirements will force you to buy a liner, but since sunken graves add to a cemetery's upkeep costs, many (though not all) cemeteries require some kind of grave liner. Check directly with local cemeteries to find out what their requirements are. Do not necessarily rely on what a funeral director tells you. If you do not wish to purchase a liner or a vault, you may be able to find a cemetery that does not require one.

Burial vaults may also be sold as a means of protecting the casket and, consequently, the remains. While some vaults may prevent water and other elements from coming in contact with the casket, they cannot prevent the decomposition of the body. Sales claims or warranties may mislead you on this point.

There are several different kinds of liners and vaults available, both sealed and unsealed. Vaults may afford more protection against water and other elements, but they cannot provide preservation. Liners are usually less expensive. Prices vary greatly according to the kind selected and the seller's markup. The cost of the unsealed concrete box or liner is in the neighborhood of $100–$200. A vault can cost $200 or more.

REMEMBER: ◆ *Know why you are buying a particular liner or vault, since, generally, the law does not require it.* ◆ *Check to see whether or not the cemetery sells liners directly. Compare its prices with those of the funeral director.* ◆ *Despite what warranties or sales materials imply or claim, sealed vaults will not provide preservation of the remains.*

Cemetery Plots, Mausoleums, and Columbaria

Funeral arrangements are only part of what must be taken care of if you select burial in a cemetery or entombment in a mausoleum after the funeral or wish to make special arrangements for cremated remains. This section discusses the options available.

Cemetery Plots

If you wish an earth burial, a cemetery plot will have to be selected and paid for (many cemeteries require that a plot be paid for in full before it is used), and there are almost as many things to keep in mind when buying a cemetery plot as when making funeral arrangements.

Just as with advance funeral planning, it is wise to take care of cemetery needs before a death occurs. You will be able to consider your choices, compare prices, get all the necessary information, and make a rational decision free from the pressures of grief and sadness. Before buying a cemetery plot, you should consider several things.

Location   You should be fairly certain where you will want to be buried. For example, you may decide that you would rather be buried in the area where you grew up or where you intend to retire, rather than in the community where you now live. You should investigate the options for reselling any plot if you decide later not to use it. Find out whether or not you can sell the plot, or whether the cemetery will buy it back from you—and at what price. Some cemeteries will permit you to exchange one plot for another in a cooperating cemetery in another location.

Size   You should also consider how large a plot to buy—one for yourself, for you and your spouse only, or for your entire family. While it is difficult, try to be realistic. If you have children, remember that they may move away and establish roots in another community and may prefer, when the time comes, to be buried there rather than where they were raised. In many cemeteries it is less expensive to purchase a double-depth grave, where caskets can be buried two deep.

Extra Costs and Restrictions   Find out not only about the actual purchase price but also about all the costs associated with a plot. Ask whether there is a charge for upkeep or for opening and closing the grave. Also find out what restrictions or requirements there are. Are you required to buy a burial vault? What type of marker is permitted? Are you permitted to place flowers on the grave? If you arrange financing for the plot, consider whether it is less expensive to have the cemetery or an outside lending institution do the financing. Often a cemetery's interest rates are higher.

When choosing a cemetery, you face the same considerations as when selecting a funeral home. Some people select a particular cemetery because it serves their religious or ethnic group. For some religious groups, for example, it is important to be buried in a cemetery with others of their faith. Other people may select a cemetery because of its convenient location or its attractiveness. Cemeteries may be operated by religious groups, nonprofit or profit-making corporations, local governments, or funeral homes. Price may also be an important consideration in choosing an establishment.

Cemetery plot prices vary greatly from one area to another, depending on the price of land and the kind of cemetery. Prices range from $100 in a small rural cemetery to more than $1,000 for a "desirable" spot in a large metropolitan area. This cost may or may not include "perpetual care," which will provide ongoing maintenance of the plot. As mentioned earlier, in addition to the plot's purchase price, there will be other charges for such items as having the grave opened, which may cost between $50 and $300. For cemeteries that require graves to be lined, you can satisfy this requirement by purchasing an inexpensive liner or an expensive burial vault. Be sure to find out what the cemetery requires before you buy the plot. Also find out whether the cemetery sells the liners or not. They may be less expensive at the cemetery than at the funeral home.

Be suspicious of high-pressure cemetery sales techniques. Don't be pressured into buying something you don't want. If you are unsure of a cemetery's reputation, check with the Better Business Bureau, a funeral director you know, or a local clergy person.

Veterans' Cemeteries

One of the death benefits available to veterans and their immediate families is burial in a national cemetery. It is not possible to reserve a space in a particular cemetery in advance, and the one closest to your home may not have space available at the time of need. If proximity to your home is not important, however, space will be made available at the nearest cemetery that is not full. The spouse and minor children of a veteran are eligible for burial in the same cemetery, but it is not possible to obtain adjoining gravesites for family members. The veteran must be buried or agree to be buried in the national cemetery in order for family members to be eligible. (Burial in Arlington National Cemetery is even more restricted.)

When filing a request for burial with the superintendent of a national cemetery, the following information will speed up the request: date of birth, branch of service and grade, Social Security number, dates of active duty, and manner of separation from the military. A funeral director can take care of filing for you, or you can do it directly.

If a veteran is not buried in a national cemetery, he or she is entitled to a $150 plot allowance from the Veterans Administration.

Mausoleums.

A plot of earth is the most commonly selected final resting place, but there are other options. Many cemeteries offer interment in mausoleums or garden crypts, where the casket and remains are placed in an above-ground building. Mausoleum space will usually be more expensive than a cemetery plot, ranging from $450 to $2,000. In addition, there may be opening and closing charges. Often the price of the space is determined by its location within the mausoleum—expensive if it is at eye or heart level, less expensive if it is near the floor or ceiling.

Columbaria and Cemetery Gardens

If cremation is selected, you are usually free to scatter the ashes as you wish, though some areas may have restrictions on where you can scatter ashes. You may prefer to place the ashes in a columbarium (a vaultlike building lined with recesses for urns) or to scatter or bury them in a cemetery garden set aside for this purpose. There will be a charge for using either space, but it will be far less than the charge for a full cemetery plot.

A niche in a columbarium is available in some areas for as little as $50. In addition to purchasing the space itself, you will have to pay extra if you wish to have an inscription on the niche.

A cemetery plot for burial of cremated remains will cost from $75 up, but, as for casket burial, there may well be additional charges for opening and closing, maintenance of the plot, and so on.

REMEMBER: ◆ *Preplanning cemetery and related arrangements, like funeral preplanning, is a good idea.* ◆ *Be sure that any plot you choose is one you will want to use when the time comes.* ◆ *Find out about all costs and regulations, including perpetual care, lot resale, markers, and grave liners, before you buy.* ◆ *Check any cemetery's reputation carefully and do not be pressured into buying anything you do not want or need.*

Markers

Most people purchase a marker or monument to mark the place of burial. Cemetery rules may dictate the kind of marker you can purchase. The two most common are the upright stone marker, often made of granite or marble, and the flat bronze or stone marker, which is flush with the ground. Traditional cemeteries have upright stone markers, while newer ones may permit only markers that are flush with the ground in order to reduce maintenance costs. Many cemeteries have both, depending on the particular section of the cemetery.

Upright markers are available in a wide range of sizes, shapes, and colors. Upright granite monuments usually start at approximately $250. The flush markers are usually less expensive. In addition to buying the marker, you will also need to pay for the lettering and the installation.

Check the cemetery regulations to see whether there are set charges or requirements for markers and their installation. Investigate the kinds of markers available at different kinds of establishments—monument dealers, cemeteries, and funeral homes. Find out in advance all the possible charges for inscription, installation, and so on, and, if possible, get them in writing.

For a veteran buried in a national cemetery, a marker is automatically provided. For a veteran buried in a private cemetery, a marker or marker allowance will be furnished upon request.

Chapter Six

PAYING FOR A FUNERAL

FUNERAL COSTS and how to meet them are important matters to consider when making funeral arrangements. Certain death benefits are available to many persons. Various prepayment or insurance plans that allow people to take care of funeral expenses in advance are also available. While it is wise to plan ahead, prepayment or burial insurance programs should be approached with a great deal of caution.

Death Benefits

The following sections discuss common death benefits.

Social Security Lump-Sum Death Payment

A payment of up to $255 for funeral expenses is available to certain survivors of persons covered by Social Security. As of August 31, 1981, this payment is available only to surviving, eligible spouses or dependent children of a deceased person entitled to the death benefit. Where there is no such survivor, payment will not be made. An application for the lump-sum payment (Form SSA8) must be filed within two years after the death of the deceased. Payment can be made either to the funeral director or to the surviving spouse or entitled child who arranged for the funeral, any of whom can file for the payment.

If you choose to pay your funeral expenses in advance, you may be able to arrange with a funeral director to prepay all but the amount of the Social Security payment. For example, on a $1,000 funeral you would prepay $745 with the remaining $255 to come from Social Security after your death.

In Canada, the Canadian Pension Plan (CPP), which is similar to the U.S. Social Security Administration, makes a lump-sum death payment for those persons covered by the plan. The amount of the payment is determined by prior contributions. More information and application forms can be obtained by contacting the local office of the CPP.

Veterans' Burial Benefits

Upon an *eligible* veteran's death, (*eligible veteran* is one who is receiving or is entitled to receive VA pension compensation) the Veterans Administration (VA) will pay a $300 funeral allowance, and if burial is not in a national cemetery, an additional $150 will be paid as a plot or interment allowance. These amounts are available for nonservice-connected deaths.

If the death is service related, an allowance of up to $1,100 will be furnished in lieu of any other burial benefit. Again the necessary papers (VA Form 21–530) must be filed within two years after the death. Payment will be made to the person who paid the burial expenses. The VA death benefit is not available for completely prepaid funerals. Thus you may wish to prepay all but the amount of the VA benefit.

Veterans and their immediate families (spouses and minor children) are entitled to burial in a national cemetery. As was noted in Chapter 5, if burial is in a national cemetery, a headstone or marker is automatically furnished. Upon request, one will also be furnished for use in a private cemetery, or a cash allowance will be provided toward the purchase of a marker if death occurred after October 18, 1979. Costs associated with transporting the remains to a national cemetery will be covered by the VA only if hospitalization or housing immediately prior to death was at a VA facility or at VA expense, if the deceased was eligible for VA disability compensation, or if the death was service connected.

Burial with military honors may also be available as a service by the staff of a local military base or installation. An American flag will be provided upon request to cover the casket of a veteran. Flags are issued at most VA offices and local post offices.

You should contact the local VA office for help with these matters, or a funeral director may be able to provide any assistance you may require.

Veterans benefits are in addition to any benefits available from Social Security.

In Canada, benefits are also available to some veterans, though coverage is not as comprehensive as in the United States. For information, contact the local office of the Department of Veterans Affairs.

Other Death Benefits

Death benefits are paid by many other groups and organizations. Civil servants and employees of certain companies, municipal governments, and railroads, for example, may be eligible for payments to help cover funeral expenses. Some unions and fraternal groups also make death benefit payments. These are usually available to a surviving relative to do with as he or she sees fit. It is not necessary to spend all the money on the funeral.

The funeral expenses of qualified indigent persons are often covered by death benefits available from state or local government social-service agencies.

REMEMBER: ◆ *You should contact the local Social Security and Veterans Administration offices to find out about eligibility for death benefits.*   ◆ *The funeral director can file for payment, or can do it directly. Sometimes the funeral director will count the benefits as a credit on the funeral bill when the payment is made directly to him or her.*   ◆ *Death benefits can be used to cover the expenses of whatever kind of disposition you arrange—burial, cremation, or whole-body donation.*

Funeral Insurance and Prepayment Options

It is only natural that many of us want to set everything in order before death, even to the point of wanting to actually prepay funeral expenses or buy some kind of funeral insurance. Plans by which funeral and cemetery expenses may be paid in advance may be appealing, but they must be examined very, very carefully. Before you sign up for any payment plan, discuss it with a lawyer, if possible, or someone else who can give you good advice. Following is a discussion of the different kinds of plans.

Prepayment Plans

Many prepayment plans (sometimes sold as insurance plans) are tied to a particular funeral home. These plans are usually the least desirable, since survivors are locked into using the services of a certain establishment. Further, the actual total price of the funeral is rarely guaranteed, so that you may needlessly tie up your money for many years.

In prearranging a funeral, a funeral director may suggest that you prepay the funeral with regular time payments. This procedure is very risky and in many states illegal if the money is not placed in a trust fund supervised by the state. If the money collected is not placed in trust, the funeral director is free to spend it at any time; nothing may be available to cover expenses upon death. Or if you die before the entire amount is paid off, the funeral home may not honor the contract. Find out what happens if you die before the plan is fully paid up. Also find out what money you get back if you decide to cancel.

You should check the reputation of any firm selling pre-need policies by contacting state authorities or the Better Business Bureau before you sign up. A funeral home may go out of business, you may move and be unable to get your money back, or your survivors may be unaware that you have prepaid funeral expenses and may make and pay for arrangements elsewhere. If the funds will not be placed in trust, prepayment should not be made under any circumstances.

The prepayment of funerals through prepayment plans or burial insurance should be considered only if the funds are adequately safeguarded (placed in trust), if the seller has a sound reputation, if you are certain you will want to use the funeral home, and if the price is guaranteed. If all these conditions are met, you may want to consider such plans, but before you sign up for anything, consider the two alternative methods of prepayment discussed next.

Special Savings Account

An excellent first step in prearranging and prefinancing your funeral is careful preplanning (the Personal Planning Forms in Appendix D can be used for this purpose). Be sure to go beyond just writing down your plans. Discuss them with those who are likely to make your funeral arrangements. If you have no close friends or family, discuss this with a clergy person, your lawyer, or a funeral director. Once you know what you want, estimate what your funeral expenses will be.

You can do this by talking with a cooperative funeral director.

Then, to provide for the cost of the funeral, establish a special savings account to cover these expenses. Because of inflation, allow an additional amount over the anticipated cost. Your deposits plus the interest earned should cover the expenses. You may desire to make the funeral home the beneficiary if you have no one else. Your bank can help you set up the account so that you retain full control during your life, with the money going to the beneficiary after your death.

The drawback to this arrangement is that, as with any other savings account, you may be tempted to use the funds for other purposes if you run short of cash. Also, it may be difficult to estimate precisely the amount to set aside. The savings account, however, does allow you complete control over your money as long as you are alive.

Insurance Policy

Like a funeral savings account, a regular life insurance policy can be taken out to cover your anticipated funeral expenses. Upon your death, the policy will provide the funds needed to cover funeral expenses.

These prepayment measures may be unnecessary if you have an estate that will cover the costs without difficulty. Also remember that there are inexpensive funeral options available even if you desire a conventional funeral. Do not let a funeral director or prearrangement salesperson talk you into prepaying for an expensive funeral unless that is what you want. Investigate immediate cremation or burial, or memorial society arrangements. These kinds of arrangements can often be obtained for little more than the amount of the widely available death benefits discussed at the beginning of this chapter.

REMEMBER: ◆ *Prepayment of funeral and cemetery expenses is to be approached very carefully.* ◆ *At the very least, be certain that the prepayment money is placed in a state-regulated trust fund.* ◆ *Think twice about plans that lock your survivors into using a particular establishment or do not guarantee a set price for the funeral.* ◆ *Be sure that any firm you deal with has a sound reputation.* ◆ *Find out what happens if you decide to cancel or if you die before the plan is fully paid up.* ◆ *If possible, have a lawyer look over any prepayment plan before you sign.* ◆ *Consider setting aside money to cover funeral expenses in a savings account, through an insurance policy, or in your estate.* ◆ *Do not overlook low-cost funeral options.*

Chapter Seven

RESOURCES

THIS CHAPTER provides a number of useful resources on funeral planning and problems often brought on by the death of a loved one. It also provides a list of books on related topics, and suggestions for a funeral consumer education program.

Additional Planning Information

A number of organizations that can provide information useful in making funeral arrangements are presented in this section. Each group may, however, have its own particular point of view, so the materials should be used with this in mind. The American Association of Retired Persons (AARP) does not specifically endorse any of these groups.

Consumer Groups
Below are the addresses of the national memorial society headquarters for the United States and Canada.

Continental Association of
 Funeral and Memorial
 Societies
1828 L Street, N.W.,
 Suite 1100
Washington, DC 20036

Memorial Society
 Association of Canada
Box 96, Station A
Weston, Ont. M9N 3M6

The names and addresses of local memorial societies are included in Appendix B. These organizations are nonprofit membership organizations dedicated to simple, low-cost, dignified funerals.

Funeral Industry Organizations

The following national funeral industry trade associations can provide you with information on funerals, though each is likely to reflect the organization's point of view. You may also want to contact a trade association if you have a complaint about a member firm.

National Funeral Directors
  and Morticians
  Association
737 West 79th Street
Chicago, IL 60620

National Funeral Directors
  Association
135 West Wells Street
Milwaukee, WI 53202

National Selected
  Morticians
1616 Central Street
Evanston, IL 60201

Order of the Golden Rule
P.O. Box 579
726 South College Street
Springfield, IL 62704

There are also state associations of funeral directors. A local funeral director can give you the correct address for the organization in your state.

The National Funeral Directors Association runs a program called Thanacap to deal with consumer complaints about funeral services. More information can be obtained by writing NFDA at the address above.

State Regulators

If you have a question about state laws or regulations, contact one of the following offices in your state capital.

The State Board of Funeral
  Directing

The State Attorney General's
  Office

The State Office of Consumer
  Affairs

Complaints about funeral-related businesses should also be directed to these offices.

Whole-Body or Organ Donation Resource Groups
The following groups can provide information on the donation of particular organs.

Deafness Research Foundation
55 East 34th Street
New York, NY 10016

Eye Bank Association of
  America
6501 Fannin Street–Suite 307
Houston, TX 77030

National Kidney Foundation
2 Park Avenue
New York, NY 10016

National Pituitary Agency
Suite 501-9
210 West Fayette Street
Baltimore, MD 21201

National Temporal Bone Bank
  Center
Massachusetts Eye & Ear
  Infirmary
243 Charles Street
Boston, MA 02114

Tissue Bank
Naval Medical Research
  Institute
National Naval Medical
  Center
Bethesda, MD 20814

The following two groups provide information on whole-body donations as well as organ donations.

Living Bank
P.O. Box 6725
Houston, TX 77005

American Medical Association
535 North Dearborn Street
Chicago, IL 60610

You should also contact the medical school to which you wish to donate in order to find out about arrangements for donation of remains.

Help with Problems

Some of the major problems faced by concerned friends and relatives of someone who is dying or recently deceased are listed below along with names of groups that may be helpful in dealing with those problems. Again, AARP provides no specific endorsements.

Living Will

Concern for Dying is a group concerned with issues related to the perhaps unwarranted prolongation of life. This group promotes a document called the Living Will, which allows you to indicate your wishes as to when you do not want heroic measures taken to prolong your life.

Concern for Dying
250 West Fifth Street
New York, NY 10019

Coping with Loss

You may wish to locate and use the counseling services offered by religious and mental health organizations in your own community. In addition, the following is a national organization devoted to death education and counseling.

Forum for Death Education
   and Counseling
P.O. Box 1226
Arlington, VA 22210

The AARP Widowed Persons Service can provide information about services available in your community. This program links the newly widowed with specially trained volunteers who themselves have been widowed.

Widowed Persons Service
AARP
1909 K Street, N.W.
Washington, DC 20049

This office can also provide copies of the "Directory of Services for the Widowed in the United States and Canada." This publication lists a wide range of service groups, including many that provide counseling. A copy of the directory can be purchased for $2.00.

The St. Francis Society is another nonprofit, nondenominational group that provides counseling in the Washington, D.C. area and distributes by mail do-it-yourself casket kits and guidance on funeral planning.

The St. Francis Burial and
  Counseling Society, Inc.
1768 Church Street, N.W.
Washington, DC 20036

Death Benefits

Contact the local Veterans Administration or Social Security field office nearest you for information and assistance.

For retired military personnel, the Retired Officers Association publishes a detailed guide called "Help Your Widow," which deals with death benefits, pensions, and so on.

Retired Officers Association
201 North Washington Street
Alexandria, VA 22314

Further Reading

There are a number of materials dealing with various aspects of death and dying. Among these are two books that present very readable, informative, and entertaining critiques of American funeral practices and the American funeral industry.

Ruth Mulvey Harmer. *The High Cost of Dying*. New York: Collier Books, 1963.

Jessica Mitford. *The American Way of Death*. New York: Fawcett World, 1963 (updated 1978).

Varying amounts of practical information can be found in the following four publications.

Consumers Union. *Funerals: Consumers' Last Rights*. Mount Vernon, New York: Consumers Union, 1977.

Yaffa Draznin. *The Business of Dying*. New York: Hawthorne Books, 1976.

Ernest Morgan. *A Manual of Death Education and Simple Burial*. Burnsville, N.C.: Celo Press, 1978. (Order from Celo Press, Burnsville, NC 28714; cost $2.00 plus postage)

Michael A. Simpson. *The Facts of Death*. Englewood Cliffs, N.J.: Prentice-Hall, 1979.

A limited list of selected references for more information follows.

Death, Dying, and the Bereavement Process

Elisabeth Kubler-Ross. *Death, the Final Stage of Growth*. Englewood Cliffs, N.J.: Prentice-Hall, 1975.

Elisabeth Kubler-Ross. *On Death and Dying*. New York: Macmillan, 1969.

Elisabeth Kubler-Ross. *Questions and Answers on Death and Dying*. New York: Macmillan, 1969.

Robert E. Neale. *The Art of Dying*. New York: Harper & Row, 1974.

Herman Feifel. *New Meanings of Death*. New York: McGraw-Hill, 1977.

Earl Grollman. *Concerning Death: A Practical Guide for the Living*. Boston: Beacon Press, 1974.

Funeral Ceremonies and Religious Practices and Beliefs

Paul Irion. *A Manual and Guide for Those Who Conduct A Humanist Funeral Service*. Baltimore: Waverly Press, 1971.

Edgar N. Jackson. *The Christian Funeral*. New York: Channel Press, 1966.

Maurice Lamm. *The Jewish Way in Death and Mourning*. New York: Jonathan David, 1969.

Corliss Lamont. *A Humanist Funeral Service*. New York: Prometheus Books, 1977.

Liston O. Mills, Ed. *Perspectives on Death*. Nashville: Abingdon, 1974.

Karl Rahner. *On the Theology of Death*. New York: Seabury, 1961.

Jack Reimer, Ed. *Jewish Reflections on Death*. New York: Schocken Books, 1974.

Richard Rutherford. *Death of a Christian: The Rite of Funerals* (Studies in the Reformed Rites of the Catholic Church). New York: Pueblo Publishing, 1981.

Cremation

Paul E. Iron. *Cremation*. Philadelphia: Fortress Press, 1968.

Widowhood

Helen Antoniak, Nancy Scott, and Nancy Worcester. *Alone*. Millbrae, Calif.: Les Femmes Publishers, 1979.

Ruth J. Loewinsohn. *Survival Handbook for Widows (and Relatives and Friends)*. Piscataway, NJ: New Century Press.

James A. Peterson. *On Being Alone.* Long Beach, Calif.:
   AARP. (Order from AARP, 215 Long Beach Blvd., Long
   Beach, CA 90801; single copy free)
Clarisa Start. *When You're a Widow.* St. Louis: Concordia,
   1968.

Organizing a Consumer Education Program

Funeral planning is a topic rarely included in programs
sponsored by church, senior citizens, or civic groups. This is
regrettable, since the purchase of funeral-related services is
one that most of us will have to make at some point. We can
benefit greatly by talking about funeral arrangements be-
forehand with friends and relatives and by obtaining reliable
information from knowledgeable persons in our community.
The Consumer Affairs section of the AARP Program Department has developed an educational program in this area
that can be used in conjunction with this planning book.
Program materials include 40 slides for a thirteen-minute
presentation, a prerecorded tape cassette, and a detailed
leader's guide. Information concerning this program can be
obtained from:

Consumer Affairs, Program Department
AARP
1909 K Street, N.W.
Washington, DC 20049.

Included in the program materials is complete information
on conducting a successful consumer education program on
funerals. When the program on funeral planning is presented, it is important that the topic of the program be
clearly stated on publicity or advance announcements, since
some people find funerals an uncomfortable subject to discuss. The emphasis on the program should be on the practical

aspects of funeral planning. No attempt should be made to promote a particular kind of funeral or a particular funeral home.

A panel presentation could serve as the focus for the meeting. The panel might consist of a local funeral director or a representative from the local funeral directors trade association, a memorial society representative, and a knowledgeable clergy person. It is very important that the panel be balanced and not simply a forum for one individual to sell services or a particular point of view. It is the responsibility of the program planners to see that this balance is achieved. The panel presentation should deal with the kinds of issues covered in this book: the range of options, legal requirements, and local prices. After the panel presentation, time should be set aside for questions and discussion.

The program might conclude with a review of the practical considerations in funeral planning. Individuals should be urged to actually do their own advance planning at home and to discuss this planning with friends, family, or appropriate professionals.

APPENDIX A

CHECKLIST FOR

SURVIVORS

IF YOU ARE FACED with having to make funeral arrangements after the death of a relative or friend, the following checklist will help you keep track of what needs to be done. Read through this checklist before doing anything else, since it will alert you to the kinds of questions you will need to ask and the decisions you will need to make. You are urged to consult the indicated portions of this planning book for more information.

Notification
Upon learning of the death, you will want to contact a number of people. If you do not wish to do this yourself, have a close relative or friend take on the task.

☐ Contact other family and friends
☐ Contact clergy
☐ Notify deceased's employer
☐ Notify deceased's or family lawyer

Preparation
Before you begin to make any arrangements, you will want to find out how much preplanning has been done and what your options might be. You may wish to check on the assistance that your local memorial society can provide (pages 13–14).

☐ Locate deceased's funeral preplanning forms, if any
☐ Contact memorial society

Disposition

You will need to call a funeral director or a disposition company to arrange for the removal of the body (pages 8–9). But before calling to arrange for the removal, you should consider what the final disposition will be: burial (page 17), cremation (pages 17–18), or donation of the body to a medical research institution (pages 18–21).

☐ Decide on kind of disposition
☐ Contact funeral director, direct disposition company, or memorial society

Ceremony

You should think about the kind of ceremony you would like to arrange and consider the most appropriate time and place for it. In thinking about the ceremony *before* you meet with a funeral director, you should consider kind of ceremony, place of ceremony, who will officiate, and so on (pages 22–26).

☐ Outline ceremony and fill in as many details or alternatives as possible

Prices

You should also think about funeral prices (pages 29–31) and specific items of merchandise needed, including kind and cost of casket (pages 49–50) and grave liner (pages 51–52), music, flowers, and other items (pages 37–40). It is a good idea to think about these items and review the information in this book *before* meeting with the funeral director so that you will have a clear sense of what you want. You may wish to contact more than one funeral home to compare prices. (See Appendix C, pages 94–103.)

☐ Ascertain merchandise and services needed
☐ Consider price decisions
☐ Compare prices at several funeral homes

Funeral Home

You will normally need to go to the funeral home to meet with the funeral director about the funeral. Take a friend, relative, or other adviser with you.

During this meeting, you will decide on many of the details of the funeral and you will probably select necessary merchandise, including a casket if one is needed. Go to the funeral home with a good sense of what you want. Review pages 5–8 for a discussion of the range of decisions you may need to make. Usually this meeting provides an opportunity to write the death notice, so it might be useful to think in advance about what you would like included.

☐ Arrange an appointment with the funeral director you have chosen
☐ Arrange to take someone with you
☐ Have a good sense of what you want
☐ Decide what should be included in the death notice

Cemetery Arrangements

Alone or with the funeral director's assistance you will need to make cemetery arrangements if there is to be an earth burial (pages 52–57).

☐ Ascertain whether the deceased owned cemetery space or whether it needs to be purchased
☐ Compare prices at several cemeteries, if a plot needs to be purchased
☐ Purchase plot if necessary
☐ Determine cemetery requirements and possible charges
☐ Make arrangements for burial or entombment

Death Benefits

The death benefits to which the deceased is entitled may include Social Security, Veterans Administration, insurance, or others (pages 58–61). Your lawyer or funeral director can assist you in filing for them.

☐ Review and file for death benefits

Other Tasks

Some of the other tasks you may need to take care of include the following.

☐ Arrange for hospitality for out-of-town guests
☐ Arrange for disposition of flowers after the funeral
☐ Keep track of expressions of sympathy for your subsequent acknowledgment
☐ Take care of the deceased's home and personal property

APPENDIX B

MEMORIAL SOCIETIES

IN THE UNITED STATES

AND CANADA

ON PAGES 79–93 IS A LISTING of memorial societies that belonged to the national associations representing funeral and memorial societies as of May, 1982. If a society near you is no longer at the address or phone number listed in the following pages, an up-to-date list of societies and their addresses can be obtained from the Continental Association of Funeral and Memorial Societies, Inc. at the address at the bottom of this page by sending a self-addressed, postage-paid envelope.

New societies are constantly being formed. If no society close to you is listed here, contact the national headquarters to find the nearest society.

Be aware, however, that just because an organization has *memorial* or *society* in its name does not mean that it is a true nonprofit memorial or funeral society. When you call, ask whether it is nonprofit and whether or not it belongs to the Continental Association of Funeral and Memorial Societies or the Memorial Society Association of Canada. You can contact the national headquarters at one of these addresses.

Continental Association of
   Funeral and Memorial
   Societies, Inc.
1828 L Street, N.W.,
   Suite 1100
Washington, DC 20036

Memorial Society Association
   of Canada
Box 96, Station A
Weston, Ont. M9N 3M6

MEMBER SOCIETIES IN THE UNITED STATES

ALABAMA

Mobile:
The Azalea Funeral and Memorial
  Council
302 Bayshore Ave., Box 92
Mobile, AL 36607
205-653-9092

ALASKA

Anchorage:
Cook Inlet Memorial Society
P.O. Box 2414
Anchorage, AK 99510
907-277-6001, 907-272-7801

ARIZONA

Phoenix:
Valley Memorial Society
1446 East 2nd Place
Mesa, AZ 85203
602-969-7449

Prescott:
Memorial Society of Prescott
335 Aubrey Street
Prescott, AZ 86301
602-778-3000

Tucson:
Tucson Memorial Society
P.O. Box 12661
Tucson, AZ 85732
602-884-5099

Yuma:
Memorial Society of Yuma
P.O. Box 4314
Yuma, AZ 85364
602-783-2339

ARKANSAS

Fayetteville:
Northwest Arkansas Memorial Society
1227 South Maxwell
Fayetteville, AR 72701
501-442-5580

Little Rock:
Memorial Society of Central Arkansas
12213 Rivercrest Drive
Little Rock, AR 72207
501-225-7276

CALIFORNIA

Arcata:
Humboldt Funeral Society
666 11th Street
Arcata, CA 95521
707-822-1321

Berkeley:
Bay Area Funeral Society
P.O. Box 264
Berkeley, CA 94701
415-841-6653

Fresno:
Valley Memorial Society
P.O. Box 101
Fresno, CA 93707
209-224-9580

Los Angeles:
Los Angeles Funeral Society, Inc.
P.O. Box 44188
Panorama City, CA 91412
213-786-6845

Modesto:
Stanislaus Memorial Society
P.O. Box 4252
Modesto, CA 95352
209-523-0316

Palo Alto:
Peninsula Funeral Society
P.O. Box 11356A
Palo Alto, CA 94306
412-321-2109

Ridgecrest:
Kern Memorial Society
P.O. Box 2122
Ridgecrest, CA 93555

Sacramento:
Sacramento Valley Memorial
  Society, Inc.
Box 161688
3720 Folsom Boulevard
Sacramento, CA 95816
916-451-4641

San Diego:
San Diego Memorial Society
P.O. Box 16336
San Diego, CA 92116
714-284-1465

San Luis Obispo:
Central Coast Memorial Society
Box 679
San Luis Obispo, CA 93406
805-543-6133

Santa Barbara:
Channel Cities Memorial Society
Box 424
Santa Barbara, CA 93102
805-962-4794

Santa Cruz:
Funeral and Memorial Society of
  Monterey Bay, Inc.
P.O. Box 2900
Santa Cruz, CA 95063
408-462-1333

Stockton:
San Joaquin Memorial Society
P.O. Box 4832
Stockton, CA 95204
209-462-8739

COLORADO

Denver:
Rocky Mountain Memorial Society
1400 Lafayette St.
Denver, CO 80218
303-830-0502

CONNECTICUT

Groton:
Memorial Society of S.E. Connecticut
Box 825
Groton, CT 06340
203-445-8348

Hartford:
Memorial Society of Greater Hartford
6 Sagamore Drive
RD #1
Simsbury, CT 06070
203-728-6609

New Haven:
Memorial Society of Greater
  New Haven
60 Connelly Parkway
c/o Co-op
Hamden, CT 06514
203-288-6463, 203-488-6511

Southbury:
Southbury Branch of Greater
  New Haven Memorial Society
974-A Heritage Village
Southbury, CT 06488
203-264-7564

Westport:
Memorial Society of S.W. Connecticut
71 Hillendale Road
Westport, CT 06880
203-227-8705

D.C.

Washington:
Memorial Society of Metropolitan
  Washington
1500 Harvard Street N.W.
Washington, DC 20009
202-234-7777

FLORIDA

Cocoa:
Memorial Society of Brevard County
P.O. Box 276
Cocoa, FL 32922
305-783-8699

DeBary:
Funeral Society of Mid-Florida
P.O. Box 262
DeBary, FL 32713
305-668-6587

Destin:
Okaloosa County & N.W. Florida
Funeral & Memorial Society
P.O. Box 7
Destin, FL 32541
904-837-6559

Ft. Myers:
Funeral & Memorial Society of S.W.
Florida, Inc.
6 E. First St., Box 6
Windmill Village
N. Ft. Meyers, FL 33903
813-995-1596

Gainesville:
Memorial Society of Alachua County
Box 13195
Gainesville, FL 32604
904-376-7073

Jacksonville:
Jacksonville Memorial Society
6915 Holiday Road N.
Jacksonville, FL 32216
904-724-3766

Miami:
Miami Memorial Society
P.O. Box 557422
Ludlam Branch
Miami, FL 33155
305-667-3697

Orlando:
Orange County Memorial Society
c/o First Unitarian Church
1815 East Robinson Street
Orlando, FL 32803
305-898-3621

Pensacola:
Funeral and Memorial Society of
Pensacola and N.W. Florida
Box 4778
Pensacola, FL 32507
904-456-7028

St. Petersburg:
Suncoast-Tampa Bay Memorial Society
719 Arlington Avenue N.
St. Petersburg, FL 33701
813-898-3294

Sarasota:
Memorial Society of Sarasota
P.O. Box 5683
Sarasota, FL 33579
813-953-3740

Tallahassee:
Funeral and Memorial Society of Leon
County
Box 20189
Tallahassee, FL 32304

Tampa:
Tampa Memorial Society
3915 North "A" Street
Tampa, FL 33609
813-877-4604

West Palm Beach:
Palm Beach Funeral Society
P.O. Box 2065
West Palm Beach, FL 33402
305-833-8936

GEORGIA

Atlanta:
Memorial Society of Georgia
1911 Cliff Valley Way, NE
Atlanta, GA 30329
404-634-2896

HAWAII

Honolulu:
Funeral and Memorial Society of Hawaii
200 North Vineyard Boulevard
Suite 403
Honolulu, HI 96817
808-538-1282

ILLINOIS

Bloomington:
McLean County Branch of Chicago
    Memorial Society
1613 East Emerson
Bloomington, IL 61701
309-828-0235

Carbondale:
Memorial Society of Carbondale Area
905 Carter Street
Carbondale, IL 62901
618-457-6240

Chicago:
Chicago Memorial Association
59 East Van Buren Street
Chicago, IL 60605
312-939-0678

Elgin:
Fox Valley Funeral Association
783 Highland Avenue
Elgin, IL 60120
312-695-5265

Peoria:
Memorial Society of Greater Peoria
908 Hamilton Boulevard
Peoria, IL 61603
309-673-5391

Rockford:
Memorial Society of N. Illinois
P.O. Box 6131
Rockford, IL 61125
815-964-7697

Urbana:
Champaign County Memorial Society
309 West Green Street
Urbana, IL 61801
217-384-8862

INDIANA

Bloomington:
Bloomington Memorial Society
2120 North Fee Lane
Bloomington, IN 47401
812-332-3695

Ft. Wayne:
Memorial Society of N.E. Indiana
306 West Rudisill Boulevard
Ft. Wayne, IN 46807
219-745-4756, 219-637-6478

Indianapolis:
Indianapolis Memorial Society
5805 East 56th Street
Indianapolis, IN 46226
317-545-6005

Muncie:
Memorial Society of Muncie Area
1900 North Morrison Road
Muncie, IN 47304
317-288-9561
(evenings) 317-289-1500

Valparaiso:
Memorial Society of N.W. Indiana
356 McIntyre Court
Valparaiso, IN 46383
219-462-5701

West Lafayette:
Greater Lafayette Memorial Society
Box 2155
West Lafayette, IN 47906
317-463-9645

IOWA

Ames:
Central Iowa Memorial Society
1015 Hyland Avenue
Ames, IA 50010
515-239-2314

Cedar Rapids:
Memorial Option Service of
Cedar Rapids
203 23rd Ave. NE
Cedar Rapids, IA 52402
319-363-3927 (evenings)

Davenport:
Blackhawk Memorial Society
3707 Eastern Avenue
Davenport, IA 52807
319-359-0816

Iowa City:
Memorial Society of Iowa River Valley
120 Dubuque Street
Iowa City, IA 52240
319-337-3019, 319-337-9828

KANSAS

Hutchinson:
Mid-Kansas Memorial Society
Woolcott Bldg., Room 310
Hutchinson, KS 67501

KENTUCKY

Lexington:
Memorial Society of Lexington, Inc.
P.O. Box 22351
Lexington, KY 40522
606-269-7788

Louisville:
Memorial Society of Greater Louisville
322 York Street
Louisville, KY 40203
502-585-5119

LOUISIANA

Baton Rouge:
Memorial Society of Greater
Baton Rouge
8470 Goodwood Avenue
Baton Rouge, LA 70806
504-926-2291

New Orleans:
Memorial Society of Greater
New Orleans
1800 Jefferson Avenue
New Orleans, LA 70115
504-891-4055

MAINE

Portland:
Memorial Society of Maine
425 Congress Street
Portland, ME 04111
207-773-5747

MARYLAND

Baltimore:
Memorial Society of Greater Baltimore
3 Ruxview Court, Apartment 101
Baltimore, MD 21204
301-296-4657, 301-488-6532

Columbia:
Howard County Memorial Foundation
10451 Twin Rivers Rd.
Wilde Lake Village
Columbia, MD 21044
301-730-7920, 301-997-1188

Greenbelt:
Maryland Suburban Memorial Society
c/o Bruce Bowman
1423 Laurell Hill
Greenbelt, MD 20770
301-474-6468

Hagerstown:
Memorial Society of Tri-State Area
15 South Mulberry
Hagerstown, MD 21740
301-733-3565

MASSACHUSETTS

Brookline:
Memorial Society of New England
25 Monmouth Street
Brookline, MA 02146
617-731-2073

New Bedford:
Memorial Society of Greater New
  Bedford, Inc.
71 Eighth Street
New Bedford, MA 02740
617-994-9686

Orleans:
Memorial Society of Cape Cod
Box 1346
Orleans, MA 02653
617-255-3841

Springfield:
Springfield Memorial Society
P.O. Box 2821
Springfield, MA 01101
413-733-7874

MICHIGAN

Ann Arbor:
Memorial Advisory and Planning
  Service
P.O. Box 7325
Ann Arbor, MI 48107
313-663-2697

Battle Creek:
Memorial Society of Battle Creek
c/o Art Center
265 East Emmet Street
Battle Creek, MI 49017
616-962-5362

Detroit:
Greater Detroit Memorial Society
4605 Cass Avenue
Detroit, MI 48201
313-833-9107

East Lansing:
Lansing Area Memorial Planning
  Society
855 Grove Street
East Lansing, MI 48823
517-351-4081

Flint:
Memorial Society of Flint
G-2474 South Ballenger Highway
Flint, MI 48507
313-232-4023

Grand Rapids:
Memorial Society of Greater
  Grand Valley
P.O. Box 1426
Grand Rapids, MI 49501

Kalamazoo:
Memorial Society of Greater
Kalamazoo
315 West Michigan
Kalamazoo, MI 49006

Mt. Pleasant:
Memorial Society of Mid-Michigan
P.O. Box 172
Mt. Pleasant, MI 48858
517-773-9548

MINNESOTA

Minneapolis:
Minnesota Funeral and Memorial
  Society
900 Mt. Curve Avenue
Minneapolis, MN 55403
612-824-2440

MISSISSIPPI

Gulfport:
Funeral and Memorial Society of the
  Mississippi Gulf Coast
P.O. Box 7406
Gulfport, MS 39501
601-435-2284

MISSOURI

Kansas City:
Greater Kansas City Memorial Society
4500 Warwick Boulevard
Kansas City, MO 64111
816-561-6322

St. Louis:
Memorial and Planned Funeral Society
5007 Waterman Boulevard
St. Louis, MO 63108
314-361-0595

MONTANA

Billings:
Memorial Society of Montana
1024 Princeton Avenue
Billings, MT 59102
406-252-5065

Missoula:
Five Valleys Burial-Memorial
   Association
401 University Avenue
Missoula, MT 59801
406-543-6952

NEBRASKA

Omaha:
Midland Memorial Society
3114 Harney Street
Omaha, NB 68131
402-345-3039

NEVADA

Las Vegas:
Funeral and Memorial Society of
   S. Nevada, Inc.
P.O. Box 1324
Las Vegas, NV 89125
702-739-6979

Reno:
Memorial Society of W. Nevada
Box 8413, University Station
Reno, NV 89507
702-322-0688

NEW HAMPSHIRE

Concord:
Memorial Society of New Hampshire
P.O. Box 702
Concord, NH 03301
603-224-8913

NEW JERSEY

Cape May:
Memorial Society of South Jersey
P.O. Box 592
Cape May, NJ 08204
609-884-8852

East Brunswick:
Raritan Valley Memorial Society
176 Tices Lane
East Brunswick, NJ 08816
201-246-9620, 201-572-1470

Lanoka Harbor:
Memorial Association of Ocean County
P.O. Box 173
Lanoka Harbor, NJ 08734

Lincroft:
Memorial Association of
   Monmouth County
1475 West Front Street
Lincroft, NJ 07738
201-741-8092

Madison:
Morris Memorial Society
Box 156
Madison, NJ 07940
201-540-1177

Montclair:
Memorial Society of Essex
67 Church Street
Montclair, NJ 07042
201-338-9510

Paramus:
Central Memorial Society
156 Forest Avenue
Paramus, NJ 07652
201-445-6008

Plainfield:
Memorial Society of Plainfield
P.O. Box 307
Plainfield, NJ 07061

Princeton:
Princeton Memorial Association
P.O. Box 1154
Princeton, NJ 08540
609-924-1604

Toms River:
Memorial Association of Ocean County
Box 1329
Toms River, NJ 08753
201-350-0228

NEW MEXICO

Albuquerque:
Memorial Association of Central New
    Mexico
P.O. Box 3251
Albuquerque, NM 87190
505-299-5384

Farmington:
Four Corners Memorial and Funeral
    Society
P.O. Box 1254
Farmington, NM 87410

Las Cruces:
Memorial and Funeral Society of
    Southern New Mexico
P.O. Box 2563
Las Cruces, NM 88001

Los Alamos:
Memorial and Funeral Society of
    Northern New Mexico
P.O. Box 178
Los Alamos, NM 87544
505-662-2346

NEW YORK

Albany:
Albany Area Memorial Society
405 Washington Avenue
Albany, NY 12206
518-465-9664

Binghamton:
Southern Tier Memorial Society
183 Riverside Drive
Binghamton, NY 13905
607-729-1641

Buffalo:
Greater Buffalo Memorial Society
695 Elmwood Avenue
Buffalo, NY 14222
716-885-2136

Clayton:
Memorial Society of Northern
    New York
RD 2, Box 321
Clayton, NY 13624
315-788-5340

Corning:
Memorial Society of Greater Corning
P.O. Box 23
Painted Post, NY 14870
607-962-2690

Ithaca:
Ithaca Memorial Society
P.O. Box 134
Ithaca, NY 14850
607-272-5476

New Hartford:
Mohawk Valley Memorial Society
28 Oxford Road
New Hartford, NY 13413
315-797-1955

New York City:
Community Funeral Society
40 East 35th Street
New York, NY 10016
212-683-4988

Consumers Memorial Society
770 Broadway
c/o Urban Community
New York, NY 10003
212-674-5400

Memorial Society of Riverside Church
490 Riverside Drive
New York, NY 10027
212-749-7000

Oneonta:
Memorial Society of Greater Oneonta
12 Ford Avenue
Oneonta, NY 13820
607-432-3491

Pomona:
Rockland County Memorial Society
Box 461
Pomona, NY 10970
914-354-2917

Port Washington:
Memorial Society of Long Island
Box 303
Port Washington, NY 11050
516-627-6590, 516-767-6026

Poughkeepsie:
Mid Hudson Memorial Society
249 Hooker Avenue
Poughkeepsie, NY 12603
914-471-5078

Rochester:
Rochester Memorial Society
220 Winton Road, S.
Rochester, NY 14610
716-461-1620

Syracuse:
Syracuse Memorial Society
P.O. Box 67
Dewitt, NY 13214
315-474-4580

Wellsville:
Upper Genesee Memorial Society
Box 274
Wellsville, NY 14895
716-593-1060

White Plains:
Funeral Planning Association of
    Westchester
Rosedale Avenue and Sycamore Lane
White Plains, NY 10605
914-946-1660

NORTH CAROLINA

Asheville:
Blue Ridge Memorial Society
P.O. Box 2601
Asheville, NC 28801

Chapel Hill:
Triangle Memorial and Funeral Society
Box 1223
Chapel Hill, NC 27514
919-942-4427

Greensboro:
Piedmont Memorial and Funeral Society
Box 16192
Greensboro, NC 27406
919-674-5501

Laurinburg:
Scotland County Funeral and Memorial
    Society
Box 192
Laurinburg, NC 28352

OHIO

Akron:
Canton-Akron Memorial Society
3300 Morewood Road
Akron, OH 44313
216-836-8094

Cincinnati:
Memorial Society of Greater
    Cincinnati, Inc.
536 Linton Street
Cincinnati, OH 45219
513-281-1564

Cleveland:
Cleveland Memorial Society
21600 Shaker Boulevard
Cleveland, OH 44122
216-751-5515

Columbus:
Memorial Society of the Columbus Area
P.O. Box 14103
Columbus, OH 43214
614-267-4696

Dayton:
Dayton Memorial Society
665 Salem Avenue
Dayton, OH 45406
513-274-5890

Toledo:
Memorial Society of N.W. Ohio
2210 Collingwood Boulevard
Toledo, OH 43620
419-475-4812

Wilmington:
Funeral and Memorial Society of
    S.W. Ohio
66 North Mulberry Street
Wilmington, OH 45177
513-382-2349

Yellow Springs:
Yellow Springs Branch of Memorial
    Society of Columbus Area
317 Dayton Street
Yellow Springs, OH 45387
513-767-2011

Youngstown:
Memorial Society of Greater
    Youngstown
75 Jackson Drive
Campbell, OH 44405
216-755-8696

OKLAHOMA

Oklahoma City:
Memorial Society of Central Oklahoma
600 NW 13th Street
Oklahoma City, OK 73103
405-232-9224

Tulsa:
Memorial Society of E. Oklahoma
2942 South Peoria
Tulsa, OK 74114
918-743-2363

OREGON

Eugene:
The Emerald Memorial Association
Box 667
Pleasant Hill, OR 97401

Portland:
Oregon Memorial Association
6220 SW 130th Street, #17
Beaverton, OR 97005
503-283-5500

PENNSYLVANIA

Bethlehem:
Lehigh Valley Memorial Society
701 Lechauweki Avenue
Bethlehem, PA 18015
215-866-7652

Erie:
Thanatopsis Society of Erie
P.O. Box 3495
Erie, PA 16508
814-864-9300

Harrisburg:
Memorial Society of Greater
  Harrisburg
1280 Clover Lane
Harrisburg, PA 17113
717-564-4761

Philadelphia:
Memorial Society of Greater
  Philadelphia
2125 Chestnut Street
Philadelphia, PA 19103
215-567-1065

Pittsburgh:
Pittsburgh Memorial Society
605 Morewood Avenue
Pittsburgh, PA 15213
412-621-8008

Pottstown:
Pottstown Branch of Memorial Society
  of Greater Philadelphia
1409 North State Street
Pottstown, PA 19464
215-323-5561

Scranton:
Memorial Society of
  Scranton-Wilkes-Barre Area
P.O. Box 212, RD #6
Clarks Summit, PA 18411
717-586-5255

RHODE ISLAND

East Greenwich:
Memorial Society of Rhode Island
119 Kenyon Avenue
East Greenwich, RI 02818
401-884-5933, 401-884-5451

SOUTH CAROLINA

Charleston:
Memorial Society of Charleston
1340 Honeysuckle Lane
Charleston, SC 29412
803-795-4429

Myrtle Beach:
Memorial Society of Eastern Carolina
P.O. Box 712
Myrtle Beach, SC 29577
803-449-6526, 803-449-3064

TENNESSEE

Chattanooga:
Memorial Society of Chattanooga
3224 Navajo Dr.
Chattanooga, TN 37411
615-899-9315

Knoxville:
East Tennessee Memorial Society
P.O. Box 10507
Knoxville, TN 37919
615-523-4176

Nashville:
Middle Tennessee Memorial Society
1808 Woodmont Boulevard
Nashville, TN 37215
615-383-5760

Pleasant Hill:
Cumberland Branch of East Tennessee
  Memorial Society
P.O. Box 246
Pleasant Hill, TN 38578
615-277-3795

TEXAS

Austin:
Austin Memorial and Burial
  Information Society
P.O. Box 4382
Austin, TX 78765

Beaumont:
Golden Triangle Memorial Society
Box 6136
Beaumont, TX 77705
713-833-6883

College Station:
Memorial Society of Bryan-College
 Station
P.O. Box 9078
College Station, TX 77840
713-696-6944

Dallas:
Dallas Area Memorial Society
4015 Normandy
Dallas, TX 75205
214-528-3990

El Paso:
Memorial Society of El Paso
P.O. Box 4951
El Paso, TX 79914
505-824-4565

Houston:
Houston Area Memorial Society
5210 Fannin Street
Houston, TX 77004
713-526-1571

Lubbock:
Lubbock Area Memorial Society
P.O. Box 6562
Lubbock, TX 79413
806-792-0367

San Antonio:
San Antonio Memorial Society
777 S.A. Bank and Trust Building
771 Navarro
San Antonio, TX 78205

UTAH

Salt Lake City:
Utah Memorial Association
569 South 13th East
Salt Lake City, UT 84102
801-582-8687

VERMONT

Burlington:
Vermont Memorial Society
P.O. Box 67
Burlington, VT 05401
802-863-4701

VIRGINIA

Alexandria:
Mt. Vernon Memorial Society
1909 Windmill Lane
Alexandria, VA 22307
703-765-5950

Arlington:
Memorial Society of Arlington
4444 Arlington Boulevard
Arlington, VA 22204
703-892-2565

Charlottesville:
Memorial Planning Society of the
 Piedmont
Edgewood Lane at Rugby Road
Charlottesville, VA 22903
804-293-8179
804-293-3133

Oakton:
Fairfax Memorial Society
P.O. Box 130
Oakton, VA 22124
703-281-4230

Richmond:
Memorial Society of Greater
 Richmond Area
Box 180
Richmond, VA 23202
804-355-0777

Roanoke:
Memorial Society of
 Roanoke Valley, Inc.
P.O. Box 8001
Roanoke, VA 24014
703-774-9314

Virginia Beach:
Memorial Society of Tidewater
P.O. Box 4621
Virginia Beach, VA 23454
804-428-1804

WASHINGTON

Seattle:
People's Memorial Association
2366 Eastlake Avenue E
Seattle, WA 98102
206-325-0489

Spokane:
Spokane Memorial Association
P.O. Box 13613
Spokane, WA 99213
509-838-5000

Yakima:
Memorial Society of
  Central Washington
P.O. Box 379
Yakima, WA 98907
(In process of joining.)

WISCONSIN

Milwaukee:
Funeral and Memorial Society
  of Greater Milwaukee
2618 Hackett Avenue
Milwaukee, WI 52311
414-332-0400

Racine:
Funeral and Memorial Society of Racine
  and Kenosha
625 College Avenue
Racine, WI 53403
414-634-0659

River Falls:
Western Wisconsin Funeral Society
110 North 3rd
River Falls, WI 54022
715-425-2052

Sturgeon Bay:
Memorial Society of Door County
c/o Hope United Church of Christ
Sturgeon Bay, WI 54235
414-743-2701

MEMBER SOCIETIES IN CANADA

ALBERTA

Calgary:
Calgary Co-op Memorial Society
28 Norseman Pl. N.W.
Calgary, Alberta T2K 5M6
403-243-5088

Edmonton:
Memorial Society of Edmonton
  and District
11447 43rd Avenue
Edmonton, Alberta T6J 0Y2
403-484-1845

Grande Prairie:
Memorial Society of Grande Prairie
P.O. Box 471
Grande Prairie, Alberta T8V 3A7

Lethbridge:
Memorial Society of Southern Alberta
924 20th Street South
Lethbridge, Alberta T1J 3J7

Red Deer:
Memorial Society of Red Deer
  and District
Box 817
Red Deer, Alberta T4N 5H2

MANITOBA

Winnipeg:
Manitoba Funeral Planning and
   Memorial Society
790 Banning St.
Winnipeg, Manitoba R3E 2H9

NEW BRUNSWICK

Fredericton:
Memorial Society of New Brunswick
P.O. Box 622
Fredericton, New Brunswick E3B 5A6

NEWFOUNDLAND

St. John's:
Memorial and Funeral Planning
   Association of Newfoundland
P.O. Box 9183
St. John's, Newfoundland A1A 2X9

NOVA SCOTIA

Halifax:
Greater Halifax Memorial Society
Box 291
Armdale, Nova Scotia B3L 4K1

Sydney:
Memorial Society of Cape Breton
P.O. Box 934
Sydney, Nova Scotia B1P 6J4

ONTARIO

Guelph:
Memorial Society of Guelph
P.O. Box 1784
Guelph, Ontario N1H 7A1
519-822-7430

Hamilton:
Hamilton Memorial Society
P.O. Box 164
Hamilton, Ontario L8N 3A2
416-549-6385

Kingston:
Memorial Society of Kingston
P.O. Box 1081
Kingston, Ontario K7L 4Y5
613-542-7271

Kitchener:
Kitchener-Waterloo Memorial Society
P.O. Box 113
Kitchener, Ontario N2G 3W9
519-743-5481

London:
Memorial Society of London
P.O. Box 1729, Station A
London, Ontario N6A 5H9

Niagara Peninsula:
Niagara Peninsula Memorial Society
Box 2102
4500 Queen Street
Niagara Peninsula, Ontario L2E 6Z2

Northern Ontario:
Memorial Society of Northern Ontario
Box 2563, Station A
Sudbury, Ontario P3A 4S9

Ottawa:
Ottawa Memorial Society
R.R. 7
62 Steeple Hill Crescent
Nepean, Ontario K2H 7V2
613-836-5630

Peterborough:
Memorial Society of Peterborough and
   District
P.O. Box 1795
Peterborough, Ontario K9J 7X6

Thunder Bay:
Memorial Society of Thunder Bay
P.O. Box 501, Station F
Thunder Bay, Ontario P7C 4W4
807-683-3051

Toronto:
Toronto Memorial Society
Box 96, Station A
Weston, Ontario M9N 3M6
416-241-6274

Windsor:
Memorial Society of Windsor
P.O. Box 481
Windsor, Ontario N9A 6M6
519-969-2252

QUEBEC

Montreal:
L'Association Funeraire de Montreal
P.O. Box 400, Station C
Montreal, Quebec H2L 4K3
514-521-2815

SASKATCHEWAN

Lloydminster:
Lloydminster, Vermillion and Districts
    Memorial Society
4729 45th Street
Lloydminster, Saskatchewan S9V oH6

Saskatoon:
Memorial Society of Saskatchewan
P.O. Box 1846
Saskatoon, Saskatchewan S7K 3S2
306-374-5190

APPENDIX C

PRICE COMPARISON

FORMS

THE FORMS INCLUDED in this section are designed to assist you in comparing the prices charged by different funeral homes, cemeteries, and monument dealers. You can do this "shopping" either in person or over the telephone when you are preplanning or after a death has occurred. In either case, be prepared with your questions. Look through this guide in advance so that you know what you want to ask.

The shopping guide contains a large number of questions. You should go through it and mark those questions related to the kind of funeral or disposition you may be interested in. Do not feel that you have to ask every question. For example, if you are not interested in cremation, there is probably little reason to ask about cremation prices. Note that many of these questions request price information for the least expensive item of service or merchandise. This is because many people are interested in inexpensive funerals, and this focus can serve as a useful way of comparing prices. But you should feel free to ask about the "average" price or, if you know about a particular item (such as a certain kind of casket), about its price.

When you contact a funeral director, explain that you are trying to obtain information on funeral home prices and offerings to help you with funeral planning. First, ask whether or not there is a prepared price list that can be sent to you. If there is, ascertaining prices will be much easier. If a price list is not available, ask the funeral director whether or not he or she has the time to answer a few questions. If the funeral director is too busy (often the case in a small establishment), ask when you may call or visit later.

Many funeral directors and cemetery operators will be very willing to cooperate with you in your attempt to solicit price information. Others may not be. This is unfortunate, but as an individual consumer there is little you can do except take this lack of cooperation into account when you make your decisions. If you are making a telephone inquiry, some funeral directors or cemetery operators may insist on talking with you in person, claiming that it is too complicated a matter to discuss on the telephone. Tell them that you have some very specific questions to which you would like answers. If he or she still insists on an in-person visit, go only if you want to, and be alert to attempts to pressure you into buying something you do not want.

As you begin to check prices, you should keep several things in mind. Any unscrupulous business person may misstate prices just to get your business. Because of inflation and other factors, prices will change over the years, so that the prices you are quoted may not be current for very long. Price is only one factor that will go into your decision about a funeral home or cemetery. You will also want to consider such things as location, reputation, and facilities.

In each form presented here, the first column contains prices from a hypothetical funeral home. *These prices are not for comparison* but are given only as an example of how to fill in the price survey. And although there is space for recording the prices of only two establishments, feel free to contact as many as you desire; use other paper or duplicate these forms to record additional information. Remember to check the prices of memorial-society plans and direct disposition companies as well as those of funeral homes.

After you complete the survey, use the information as a guide in planning the type of funeral you want on the forms in Appendix D.

FUNERAL HOME PRICES

	Name of Funeral Home	Name of Funeral Home	Name of Funeral Home
	*Community		

Do you use package pricing or the itemization pricing method? (Proceed to appropriate section.)

ITEMIZATION

1 What is the cost for
(Ask only about the things you are interested in.)

removal of remains?	$ 45 w/l 50 mi		
embalming?	$ 75		
use of the chapel?	$ 55 for service		
use of the viewing room?	$ 25 for 3 hrs.		
arranging for the death notice?	no charge		
church services?	$ 35		
a burial permit?	$ 7		
death certificates?	$ 3 each		
use of the hearse?	$ 42 w/l 50 mi		
filing for death benefits?	$ 15		
use of one limousine?	$ 45 w/l 50 mi		
use of each additional limousine?	$ 45		
the services of your professional staff?	$ 275		
a grave liner?	$ 105 least expensive		
a vault or interment receptacle?	$ 215 (vault)		

* Prices shown are not for comparison with prices in your area

FUNERAL HOME PRICES

	Name of Funeral Home	Name of Funeral Home	Name of Funeral Home
	Community		
burial clothing?	$ 37 (gown)		
a flower car?	$ 35		
an organist?	$ 15		
a soloist?	$ 15		

2 What is the cost of your least expensive casket (or the particular one you are interested in)**?**

What kind is it?

$ 125		
cloth-covered wood		

3 What is the cost of (List other items you are interested in.)

police escort	$ 25		
nurse	$ 35		

4 Last year, what was your average charge for a funeral including embalming, viewing, and so on?

$ 1750 approx.		

PACKAGE PRICING

1 What is the cost of your lowest-priced funeral?

$ 985		

FUNERAL HOME PRICES

	Name of Funeral Home	Name of Funeral Home	Name of Funeral Home
	Community cloth-covered wood		

2 What type of casket is used?
(If you wish to find out about a package price for a funeral with a particular casket, ask for that package price.)

3 What is the price reduction if I wish to decline

embalming?	$50		
use of the viewing room?	$25		
use of the chapel facilities for ceremony?	$40		
use of a limousine?	$35		

4 What other items can one decline, and what price reduction will be given? (List.)

music (taped)	$15		
guestbook	$5		

DIRECT BURIAL

Do you offer a direct burial (no viewing)?
(If so,)

| | *Yes* | | |

1 What is your lowest charge?

| | $275 | | |

FUNERAL HOME PRICES

	Name of Funeral Home	Name of Funeral Home	Name of Funeral Home
	Community		

2 If this is not all-inclusive, what are additional items (List.) **and what do they cost?**

cemetery expenses	approx $375		

CREMATION

Do you offer cremation?
(If so,)

Yes		

1 What is the lowest charge for direct cremation (no viewing) **using a cremation container?**

$295		

2 What is the lowest charge for cremation after viewing?

$495		

3 Are there any extra charges? (If so,) **what are they and how much?** (List.)

actual cremation	$95		
death certificates	$3 each		

4 What is the lowest cost for an urn or other receptacle for cremated remains?

What kind is it?

$75 single container bronze like color		

CEMETERY PRICES

	Name of Cemetery	Name of Cemetery	Name of Cemetery
	* Pine Cemetery		

CASKET BURIAL

1 What is the lowest price for adult-size grave space for a single grave?

$ 375

double (side-by-side) grave?

$ 650

double-depth grave?

$ 475

2 Is a perpetual care cost included in plot purchase?

Yes

(If not,) **what are the charges?**

3 What is the fee for opening and closing the grave?

$ 150 (weekdays)

4 Is there an extra fee for Saturday, Sunday, or holiday opening and closing? (If so,) **how much?**

$ 50

5 Is a grave liner required?

Yes

6 Do you sell liners?

Yes

7 What is the cost of the least expensive liner?

$ 155

* Prices shown are not for comparison with prices in your area.

CEMETERY PRICES

	Name of Cemetery	Name of Cemetery	Name of Cemetery
	Pine Cemetery		

ENTOMBMENT

Do you have a mausoleum? — yes

(If so,)
1 What is the lowest price for a

single crypt? — $585

double-depth crypt? — none

side-by-side crypt? — 2 x $585

2 What is the entombment fee? — $125

3 What is the inscription cost if it is not included in the entombment fee? — $7.50 per letter

BURIAL OF CREMATED REMAINS

Do you offer grave space for cremated remains? — Yes
(If so,)

1 What is the charge? — $105

2 How much is the opening and closing fee? — $50

3 Is a grave liner necessary? (If so,) **how much does it cost?** — not necessary

COLUMBARIUM FACILITIES

Do you have a columbarium? — Yes

CEMETERY PRICES

	Name of Cemetery	Name of Cemetery	Name of Cemetery
	Pine Cemetery		
1 (If so,) **What is the charge for a** single niche?	$75		
double niche?	$125		

SCATTERING OF ASHES

Do you scatter ashes? (If so,)	Yes		
1 What is the charge?	$50		

MARKERS

Do you sell markers? (If so,)	Yes		
1 What is the lowest price for a standard, single-grave marker, inscription included?	$400		
2 Please describe the size and material.	flush, approx 2×3 ft. granite		
3 Is there an installation fee?	not if purchased from us		
(If so,) **how much is it?**			
4 What is the installation fee if the marker is purchased elsewhere?	$150		
5 What is the lowest charge for a double or companion marker?	$690		
6 Are there any restrictions as to markers? (If so,) **what?**	Limitation on size & design		

MONUMENT DEALER PRICES

	Name of Dealer	Name of Dealer	Name of Dealer
	* *Peace Monuments*		

1 What is the lowest price for a standard single (or double) marker with inscription?

single $475

2 (For a double marker) is the second inscription included in the price? (If not,) what is the cost?

Yes

3 What material is used for the lowest-priced marker? What size is it? What kind of inscription is included?

granite

Upright

Name & date

* Prices shown are not for comparison with prices in your area.

APPENDIX D

PERSONAL PLANNING

FORMS

YOU CAN USE THESE FORMS to record your wishes for your own funeral. They will guide your survivors when they have to make arrangements. They will not, however, take the place of a will. Be sure to discuss your wishes with close family or friends as well as putting them down in writing. *Do not lock the only copy of these instructions away in a safe-deposit box or vault*, since the box may not be opened until after your funeral.

You are free to duplicate these forms. Give one copy of the instructions to the person who is likely to make arrangements for you. It would also be wise to keep one copy of the forms in a place where your survivors can easily find it upon your death. And you may wish to give your clergy person a copy.

You can also use these forms as a first step in preplanning your own funeral if you are going to arrange for prepayment. (Again, all prepayment plans should be carefully investigated and agreed to only after you are sure of what you are getting.)

Finally, if you are making funeral arrangements immediately following a death, you can use these forms in conjunction with the Checklist for Survivors (Appendix A) as a further listing of things to think about before you go to the funeral home. Your best assurance of getting what you want is to know what you want before you begin making funeral and related arrangements.

Fill out only those sections of the personal planning forms that you wish to complete. Remember that these forms do not take the place of a will. You may also want to record more information than these forms call for. Following is an excellent document—which can be obtained from the given address—that provides space to record a wide range of important information, from stock holdings to dates of military service.

"Your Vital Papers"
Cost, $3.95 (Price Subject
to Change Without Notice)

Action for Independent
    Maturity
1909 K Street, N.W.
Washington, DC 20049

PERSONAL PLANNING FORMS

PERSONAL INFORMATION

1 Name: _____

Maiden Name : _____

2 Address: _____

STREET

_____

CITY   STATE   ZIP CODE

3 Social Security Number: _____

4 Place of Birth: _____ **5** Date of Birth: _____

6 Citizenship: _____

7 Father's Name: _____

Place of Birth: _____ Date of Birth: _____

8 Mother's Maiden Name: _____

Place of Birth: _____ Date of Birth: _____

9 Marital Status: _____

Spouse's Name: _____

10 Occupation: _____

11 Employer: _____

12 Previous Occupations or Employers: _____

_____

13 Religious Affiliation: _____

Local Congregation: _____

Clergy Person: _____

14 Military Service:

Branch: _____   Dates of Service: _____

Service Number: _____   Manner of Separation: _____

LEGAL, FINANCIAL, AND OTHER INFORMATION FOR SURVIVORS

15 The persons listed below should be called upon my death.

Name	Relationship	Address	Telephone

16 My lawyer is _____

_____

17 My accountant is _____

_____

18 The executor of my estate is _____

_____

_____

19 I have accounts at the following banking institutions.

Name	Address	Type	Number

20 I have credit accounts with the following companies.

Name	Address	Account Number

21 I have the following insurance policies.

Type	Policy Number	Company

PERSONAL PLANNING FORMS

22 My will is located at _____

23 My safe-deposit box number is _____, located at _____

_____

_____

24 The key to my safe-deposit box is located at _____

FUNERAL ARRANGEMENTS

25 I have made contacts with the following organizations or companies regarding funeral arrangements.

_____ Memorial Society

_____
NAME

_____
ADDRESS

_____
TELEPHONE NUMBER

_____ Funeral Home

_____
NAME

_____
ADDRESS

_____
TELEPHONE NUMBER

_____ Disposition Company

_____
NAME

_____
ADDRESS

_____
TELEPHONE NUMBER

26 _____ I have not prepaid my funeral expenses.

_____ I have prepaid my funeral expenses through the following plan.

_____
NAME

_____
ADDRESS

_____
PLAN OR POLICY NUMBER

PERSONAL PLANNING FORMS

27 I have not made arrangements with any particular firm, but I suggest that the following funeral home, memorial society, or disposition company be called upon my death.

_____

NAME

_____

ADDRESS

DISPOSITION AND SERVICE

28 Place of Disposition

_____ I wish to be buried at _____ Cemetery.

I own space number _____

_____ I wish my remains entombed at _____

I own crypt number _____

_____ I wish my remains to be cremated and

☐ scattered (if permitted) at _____

☐ buried at _____ Cemetery.

I own space number _____

☐ placed in a columbarium niche at _____

I own niche number _____

_____ I have arranged for donation of my body to the following institution.

_____

NAME

_____

ADDRESS

NOTE: Attach to these planning forms a copy of your arrangement for whole-body donation.
If my donation is not accepted, I desire as an alternative the kind of funeral and disposition indicated with the abbreviation ALT.

PERSONAL PLANNING FORMS

_____ In addition to the disposition marked above, I wish to donate the following tissues or organs (or any needed parts) for the purpose of transplantation or other medical uses.

NOTE: Be sure to complete a donor card as described on pages 22-23.

_____

_____

_____ I prefer the following disposition to any of the above. *(such as burial at sea)*

_____

29 _____ I prefer no service.

_____ I prefer the following type of service.

☐ Memorial service without the body present

☐ Service with the body present and everyone welcome to attend

☐ Service with the body present and only close family and friends attending

30 _____ I prefer no calling hours or viewing before the service.

_____ I have no objection to calling hours or viewing before the service.

31 I wish to have the service take place at _____

32 I wish to have _____ or _____ officiate.

In addition, I wish the following persons to take part, if possible.

_____

_____

_____

_____

_____

PERSONAL PLANNING FORMS

33 I would like the following included in the service.

Readings _____

_____

Scripture _____

_____

Prayers _____

_____

Music _____

_____

Other _____

_____

34 I would like to have the following six persons serve as pallbearers.

a. _____

b. _____

c. _____

d. _____

e. _____

f. _____

35 I would like the following fraternal services conducted for me.

_____

_____

PERSONAL PLANNING FORMS

36 I prefer that the casket be

_____ open for viewing before the service.

_____ open during the service.

_____ open only for close family and friends.

_____ closed at all times.

FLOWERS AND MEMORIAL GIFTS

37 I prefer that flowers

_____ not be sent at all.

_____ be sent only by immediate family.

_____ be sent by all who desire to do so.

38 I request that memorial gifts be given to the following group(s) in my memory.

_____

_____

_____

ADDITIONAL FUNERAL ITEMS AND INSTRUCTIONS

39 _____ I prefer no embalming.
NOTE: This will usually preclude public viewing of the remains.

40 I wish to be buried in _____
(If you have a preference, specify the particular clothing you wish used.)

41 I prefer

_____ an inexpensive casket.

_____ an expensive casket.

42 I prefer the following kind of casket.

_____ cloth-covered softwood

_____ hardwood

_____ nonsealer metal

_____ sealer metal

I have the following specific preferences for color, style, price range.

_____

43 I prefer

_____ the least expensive grave liner that will satisfy any existing requirements.

_____ a more expensive burial vault.

I have the following specific preferences for a grave liner or vault.

_____

44 _____ I prefer no marker.

_____ I prefer the following kind of marker (check with your cemetery to find out its requirements).
  □ stone, upright

  □ stone, flush with ground

  □ metal, flush with ground

I have the following specific preferences with regard to material, shape, or inscription.

_____

_____

_____

PERSONAL PLANNING FORMS

DEATH NOTICES

45 _____ I prefer no death notice.

_____ I prefer a death notice, which I wish to appear in the following papers.

_____

_____

_____

The following information, in addition to that in the Personal Information section, may be helpful in preparing a death notice.

46 Residences, including number of years:

_____

_____

47 Education (degrees and granting institutions):

_____

_____

48 Organizational Affiliations:

Name   Offices Held

_____   _____

_____   _____

_____   _____

49 Military commendations and civic honors: _____

_____

50 Other: _____

PERSONAL PLANNING FORMS

ADDITIONAL INSTRUCTIONS

_____

_____

_____

_____

_____

_____

_____

_____

_____

_____

_____

_____

_____

_____

_____

_____

_____

_____

_____

_____

_____

_____

PERSONAL PLANNING FORMS

ADDITIONAL INSTRUCTIONS

_____

_____

_____

_____

_____

_____

_____

_____

_____

_____

_____

_____

_____

_____

_____

_____

_____

_____

_____

_____

_____

_____

_____

Fight inflation 5 ways as a member of AARP

Like most people these days, you're probably more and more concerned about inflation and its impact on your budget.

That's why AARP has developed a whole series of money-saving services. They can help you fight back against inflationary increases in pharmacy prices, insurance premiums, travel costs and more.

And these services are just one facet of AARP membership. You also receive *Modern Maturity*, the fascinating bimonthly members magazine, and the informative *News Bulletin*.

Perhaps most important of all, you are represented whenever and wherever legislators are deciding on issues that will affect you—including pension reform, Social Security, and the cost of medical care.

Join AARP now, and you'll be able to fight inflation five ways:

- *Save on prescriptions and health aids through the non-profit Pharmacy Service.*
- *Enjoy substantial discounts on hotels, motels and rental cars through the Purchase Privilege Program.*
- *Save on health insurance with AARP's group rates.*
- *Earn high interest, without tying up your money, when you participate in the Association's money market fund.*
- *Make sure you're claiming all your deductions with the help of the Tax-Aide Program (you may even want to become a Tax-Aide volunteer).*

It's all yours for only $5 a year when you join AARP. And anyone age 55 or over—retired or not—is invited to join.

Simply send your check for $5 (includes membership for your spouse also) to:

American Association of Retired Persons
Membership Department
215 Long Beach Boulevard
Long Beach, CA 90801